UNSTOPPABLE
LEADERSHIP AND EXPONENTIAL RESULTS

Bjorn Christian Martinoff and
Victoria Penaflor Martinoff

Illustrations by Rene Trinidad Aldonza
Graphics by Rosario Laperal

Copyright © 2018

CONTENTS

PRAISE	ix
GRATITUDE	1
FOREWORD	3
PREFACE	7
INTRODUCTION	13
WHAT IS POWER? POWER VERSUS FORCE AND MANAGEMENT VERSUS LEADERSHIP	15
WHAT IS LEADERSHIP?	23
THE FORMULA FOR SUCCESS	25
FROM REGULAR GROWTH TO EXPONENTIAL GROWTH	29
GROWTH ONLY HAPPENS OUTSIDE OF THE COMFORT ZONE	35
MEASURING GROWTH ON THE POWER SCALE	37
THE 3.5 STAGES OF GROWTH	39
THE HIGHEST BARRIERS TO INDIVIDUAL GROWTH	45
WHAT SLOWS DOWN YOUR LEADERSHIP TEAM	49
BREAKDOWN BEFORE BREAKTHROUGH	57

CONTENTS

THE EVOLUTIONARY STAGES IN DEVELOPING LEADERS	59
EXPONENTIAL BREAKTHROUGH LEADERSHIP	63
VECTORING ENERGY ADDED TO FORMULA = TEAM SUCCESS FORMULA	75
BUCKETS OF ENERGY	89
CRAFTING YOUR PURPOSE	93
CRAFTING YOUR VISION	97
ARTICULATING YOUR VALUES	117
TIMING OF GROWTH INTERVENTIONS AND WHY MOST CHANGE EFFORTS FAIL	129
THE 6 + 1 DRIVERS OF ENGAGEMENT	131
FINAL WORDS	137
OTHER HELPFUL TOPICS	139
ABOUT THE AUTHORS	153
MORE PRAISE	155

Copyright © 2018 by Bjorn Christian Martinoff.
And Maria Victoria Penaflor Martinoff

Illustrations by Rene Trinidad Aldonza
Graphics by Rosario Laperal

All rights reserved.

No part of this publication may be reproduced, stored in a retrieval system, or transmitted in any form or by any means, electronic, mechanical, photocopying, recording, scanning, or otherwise, except as permitted under Section 107 or 108 of the 1976 United States Copyright Act, without either the prior written permission of the Publisher, or authorization through payment of the appropriate per-copy fee to the Publisher.

Requests to the Publisher for permission should be addressed to the Permissions Department, FIC International, 9719 Pililia Street #201, Makati City, Philippines, 1208, info@fortune100coach.com

Limit of Liability/Disclaimer of Warranty: While the publisher and authors have used their best efforts in preparing this book, they make no representations or warranties concerning the accuracy or completeness of the contents of this book and specifically disclaim any implied warranties of merchantability or fitness for a particular purpose. No warranty may be created or extended by sales representatives or written sales materials. The advice and strategies contained herein may not be suitable for your situation. You should consult with a professional where appropriate. Some or all of the material here may have been published in other media before, examples are not limited to internet, blogs, websites, print, magazines, etc. Neither the publisher nor authors shall be liable for any loss of profit or any other damages, commercial or otherwise, including but not limited to special, incidental, consequential, or other damages.

Printed in the Philippines 2018
ISBN: 978-0-692-92656-7

To our children, may you live lives that inspire you.

Unstoppable Leadership and Exponential Results

PRAISE FOR UNSTOPPABLE LEADERSHIP AND EXPONENTIAL RESULTS

Wow! I thought I would glance at the book so I could muse on it for a few days and I ended up reading through the book. I could literally not put it down! The ideas are insightful and inspiring (e.g., power vs. force vs. empowerment), but the communication of ideas through artwork is stunning. What a tour de force!

Dave Ulrich
Partner at the RBL Group and
Rensis Likert Professor at the Ross School
of Business of the University of Michigan

It's never too late for leaders to embrace empowerment and effectively employ it in their organizations. It makes the organization nimble and agile besides bringing an entrepreneurial mindset amongst the teams—all of which power growth. The Martinoffs bring out these leadership concepts brilliantly in this book with strong examples and insights synthesized from their vast experience. This book serves as a good guide to unleash the energy in your teams and transform yourself into the realm of being "unstoppable" to deliver exponential growth.

Sanjiv Mehta
Executive Vice President at Unilever South Asia

This book is inspiring and hard to put down. It refocuses our purpose and prepares us to lead in the new age of a fast-changing world in a realistic and practical way. It provides guidance on how to go outside one's comfort zone to continue to evolve as a leader and how to better lead our life as well as the organizations and people with whom we have been entrusted. This book is a must-read for any aspiring leader who wants to take their capabilities to the next level!

Cherrie Mckenzie
GBS General Manager for Emerging Markets at Goodyear Regional Business Services

This is both a practical and an inspirational guide to becoming a more powerful leader and human being! Bjorn's and Victoria's storytelling coupled with simple exercises provides life-changing insights for being your best self at your work and in your personal life.

Steven Gross
Human Resources Vice President at Unilever North Africa, Middle East, Turkey, Russia, Ukraine and Belarus

I enjoyed Bjorn's and Victoria's book—particularly the part about building a purpose-centered organization.

Robert Hargrove
Chief Executive Officer of Consigliere, the author and Chief Executive Officer of the Titans Playbook and Billion Dollar Coach

GRATITUDE

IT TAKES A village to raise a child, and it takes a small village to put together a book. All of us are standing on the shoulders of giants. It is now up to us to take what these giants have created and take it to the next level. So, I want to thank all the wise men and women of the past who have shared their wisdom with us and have influenced us. This book is in honor of them.

I also want to thank my many teachers, friends, clients and mentors who have taught me, from whom I have learned and who mentored me over the course of my life. Many have stood by me and have been wonderful supports over the years and decades. I cannot express how much this has all meant to me on my own journey to empowerment. Without these people, my life would not be what it is today.

I am forever grateful especially to Stephen Smythe who was my boss at Mercedes-Benz, to Jerry Perez de Tagle who gave me a chance in consulting and to Tony Robbins who taught me my first coaching lessons. I am grateful to Eileen Tupaz, my ever-brilliant and supportive editor; Rene Trinidad Aldonza, who did the beautiful and amazing illustrations; and Rosario Laperal, the graphic designer who did all the wonderful graphics for this book.

Special gratitude also goes to my wife for co-authoring this book and supporting me along the way, and to our children who have been incredibly supportive and patient during the time it took to put this book together.

I am also grateful to my parents who helped shape the young me to become who I am today. Mostly, I wish to thank my higher power for all the support, encouragement and inspiration. It's been a true blessing.

FOREWORD

Is there a formula to achieving exponential results? What is the recipe that combines disparate ingredients into an inspirational leader?

For answers, read Bjorn and Victoria Martinoff's book *Unstoppable Leadership and Exponential Results*. I met Bjorn over 15 years ago when he was starting his journey of exploration on the importance of living as a human "being" rather than a human "doing". Most of us focus on success, happiness, wealth, health or any number of worldly markers of achievement. We believe that doing certain actions will lead to these results which will then enable us to be happy.

Bjorn explained to me when I first met him that the process is actually the other way round. When you focus on your being—on *being* compassionate, generous, loving, forgiving, warm, diligent, committed, honest, etc.—then you automatically do certain things and behave in a way that gets you the desired results. So the process is actually Be-Do-Have and not Have-Do-Be. These concepts are simple but layered and Bjorn, in his earlier book *Develop Exponential Power: Stop Chasing It and Let It Chase You* and now this new book *Unstoppable Leadership and Exponential Results*, has disaggregated the concepts and the formula into simple steps that can be understood and applied at both an individual and organizational level. In the process, the distinction between power and force, management and leadership and the role of energy become clear.

In this book, Bjorn and Victoria explain the success formula and the multiplier effect that leads to exponential growth. The illustrations and graphics scattered through the book aid reading and comprehension. It's a pleasure to see how Bjorn in partnership with Victoria has used his experience as a coach to global chief executive officers to distill insights that—when fully assimilated and consistently applied—can explain to each one of us how to be "unstoppable" in leading with power and delivering exponential results.

Anjali Raina
Executive Director
India Research Center
Harvard Business School

Author's Biography: Anjali Raina serves as an Executive Director of the India Research Center at Harvard Business School. Ms. Raina spent 15 years at Citigroup India where she served as the Country Training Director. She was responsible for training, development and change management for the consumer bank as well as for Citigroup's associates and affiliate companies in India. She was also on the Citi Bank management committee and provided training resources throughout the Asia-Pacific region. Prior to Citigroup India, she worked for more than a decade at ANZ Grindlays Bank PLC. She has been a Non-Executive Independent Director at Mahindra

Insurance Brokers Ltd. since March 2015 and also serves as an Independent Director at Mahindra Rural Housing Finance Ltd. Ms. Raina earned a master's degree from the Indian Institute of Management, Calcutta, in 1981 and a bachelor's degree from Loreto College in the University of Calcutta in 1979.

PREFACE

AS A CHILD, I was shy, introverted and insecure. The shyness and introversion were natural. The insecurity was the result of being told over and over again that I didn't possess the qualities that were necessary to "making it" in life.

While none of this seems like a promising start to living a successful life, it set me off on what would eventually turn out to be a life-long quest. Having felt so weak, timid and anxious as a child, I was deeply interested in acquiring strength, confidence, and assurance. In a word, I was interested in *power*.

In my search, I scoured books and attended classes, seminars and workshops. In the process, I realized two things: (1) the rest of the world was as *interested* in power as I was; and (2) the rest of the world was as *confused* about power as I was.

What do I mean when I say confused?

Simply this: power, as it was variously described in the literature and by the experts, appeared contradictory. On the one hand, it's supposed to be *empowering*. It's supposed to enliven, embolden, energize, encourage and enable. On the other hand, so many of the techniques employed on its behalf appear to be *disempowering*—strategies involving deception, duplicity, falsification, manipulation, and so on and so forth. I wanted power so I could empower myself and others, but the kind of power I kept reading or hearing about in my search occurred to me as disempowering and diminishing. That is, it left me demoralized, disappointed and disillusioned.

After much reflection, it began to occur to me that the confusion was coming from using the same word to label two startlingly different phenomena. The empowering kind of power that I was interested in—which gave people a choice, freedom and self-respect—was what I eventually decided to call Power. The disempowering kind that involved deception, duplicity, falsification, manipulation, and so on and so forth—and which took away people's choice, freedom, and self-respect—was what I eventually decided to call Force. It also occurred to me that people only resorted to Force and its tactics when they didn't have the knowledge, patience or skill to cultivate genuine Power.

After distinguishing these two, I set out to discover if other people could perceive the distinction the same way I did. In my encounters with audiences both large and small, I asked people how they felt when they were being forced and what happened to their energy when they were being forced. What I found out was that about 99 percent of people dislike being forced, and, that *100 percent* of people feel their energy *decreasing* when they're being forced.

I was blown away by that discovery. It allowed me to refine my original distinctions and to fine-tune my earlier search. If Force *decreases* energy, Power, as its opposite, *increases* energy. Hence, searching for Power essentially boils down to searching for ways of being in the world that *increase* energy.

With this level of clarity about what I was looking for, I was able to identify 28 major ways of being in the world that increase our personal energy and the energy of others—ways of being such as Alignment, Confidence, Determination, Focus and Integrity. These ways of being that generate Power became the subject of my first book *Develop Exponential Power: Stop Chasing It and Let It Chase You*. I highly recommend you get yourself a copy.

Over time, however, I began to discover that practicing these empowering ways of being *together* led to a generation of power that was far beyond "the sum of the parts." When this collectively greater power is then used for a clearly-articulated higher purpose, it leads to massive growth. This then became the subject of this book *Unstoppable Leadership and Exponential Results*.

As you can imagine, this discovery paved the way for further discoveries. Not too long after I'd answered the question of Power versus Force for myself, a new question emerged: What did this distinction imply for how the world's companies are being run? With observation and reflection, a new distinction revealed itself to me—the distinction between Leadership and Management.

Just like before, I set out to discover if this new distinction could be perceived by other people as well. As I questioned the people I met, a shocking 95 percent of them associated Leadership with Power and Management with Force. In short, the majority of the world's companies are being run *in a way that causes energy to decrease*—a highly undesirable and unsustainable state of affairs given that, more than ever, businesses need to achieve so much more with so much less.

It's to address this state of affairs that I've decided to write this new book with my wife Victoria. We simply *cannot* afford the costs of decreased energy in the workplace. We need all the energy that we can generate to thrive in the face of escalating competition, higher costs and fewer resources.

In fact, we cannot afford the costs of decreased energy *beyond* the workplace. We also need the energy to address the pressing and urgent issues confronting our families, our communities, our societies and our countries. The presence of Force rather than Power and the predominance of Management over Leadership is a concern that affects us both personally and globally.

Our world is changing quickly. Global weather, economy, politics and more are shifting rapidly. Come to think of it, there isn't much that isn't changing and changing all the time. Major shifts used to occur every 209 years, and then that accelerated to every 20 years, and then that accelerated to two months, and now it's accelerating perhaps every few days. In the past, we could rely on there being a lull between storms, but that's no longer the case. Change is coming like a wildly raging storm, transforming everything in its path. Today, businesses are shutting down, restaurant chains are being abandoned and entire industries disappear as consumer tastes and desires evolve. Some of the world's biggest and most famous companies like Sony are struggling to stay relevant and car manufacturers have failed to listen to the market, losing opportunities to smaller and more agile competitors. Silicon Valley is a prime example of constant, consistent and ever-accelerating change, always trying to catch up or stay ahead.

Now, while change and transformation can be exciting, they can also induce fear. Fear slows us down. Surprisingly, even at the executive levels, fear can take root. It can remain high especially during unusual times (and when was the last time things were normal?). The biggest changes are still to come. Artificial intelligence (AI) is right around the corner and accelerating toward us. AI will do many things better than humans and today's supercomputers are already outperforming us by an ever-widening margin.

In the past, we would train people to become assembly line workers. Those jobs are gone. In this ever-changing world, can we afford to do what we have always done and how we have always done things? Individual human beings don't have the capacity any longer to compete with computers, and supercomputers are now building network connections to other computers, multiplying their computing speed and bandwidth. In short, these machines are getting further and further ahead. As we humans fall behind, we need to become both more flexible and creative. We need to be wise and to understand how to succeed in the face of these conditions.

Just like supercomputers and the information

technology industry, we humans need to continue to develop ourselves and to become smarter, more flexible and more creative. Most of all, we need to learn to work together at a level never before known or considered.

Because of all this, Victoria and I wrote this book. Our intention is to inspire our readers to begin to replace the culture of Force and Management that's currently in place with a culture of Power and Leadership. While our book doesn't present all the answers, it does pose *the* question. And to our mind, presenting answers can easily devolve into Force while asking questions ultimately contributes to unleashing Power.

We hope this book unleashes yours.

INTRODUCTION

ALTHOUGH THIS IS a book about leadership, power and results, its contents are structured around energy. It is easy to see that when we plug a device into the wall what we get is power. It is not so easy to see how that relates to a human being.

Why?

Quite simply, it's because power without energy is pointless. If you owned a McLaren race car with 1000 horsepower but had no fuel in it, all that potential (horsepower) would remain exactly as it is—*just* potential. Without the energy (the fuel) plus a spark, that racecar won't go anywhere on its own. Instead, you may have to tow it around in a truck or trailer (and doesn't it sometimes feel like that's what we are doing with employees?). Instead of them being self-motivated, we seem to have to drag them along. This is hardly fun and highly unproductive.

But even a racecar with fuel and spark wouldn't be of any use if all that power is going in the wrong direction.

For this reason, Victoria and I can't write a book about

leadership, power and results without also writing about purpose, vision and alignment.

In short, everything is necessary for the drive to even happen.

Later parts of this book will be about the practical aspects of making this all work. After all, we are after results.

Now, just as the terms and meanings of Power and Force are distinct, the terms Leader and Follower are distinctions based on roles, not distinctions based on *personalities*. Most people in organizations act as both Leaders and Followers. Even a chief executive officer is a Follower—he's accountable to the board of directors.

So, as you read the different parts of this book, keep those distinctions in mind.

We are committed that by the end of this book, you'll have everything that you need to empower your purpose and drive your results.

As Paulo Coelho once put it, "A life without cause is a life without effect."

Enjoy reading!

WHAT IS POWER? POWER VERSUS FORCE AND MANAGEMENT VERSUS LEADERSHIP

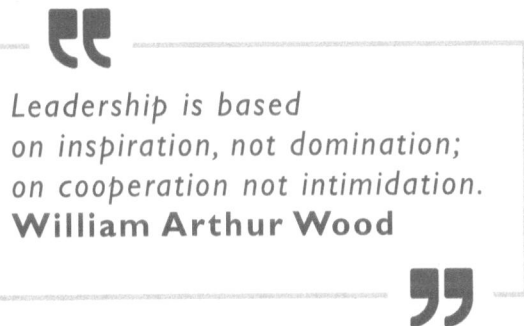

> *Leadership is based on inspiration, not domination; on cooperation not intimidation.*
> **William Arthur Wood**

AT THE EVERYDAY level of conversation and understanding, power, and sometimes leadership, has gotten a bad rap. It has often been confused with force, manipulation or worse. This deserves clarification. Power in our context deserves to be redeemed and refers in this writing to our ability to influence ourselves primarily, and our environment and the behavior of other people secondarily. It's about getting things done. Hundreds of books have been written on the subject—books whose success in the market testifies to a deeply felt need we all have to gain or develop power in ourselves.

As leaders it is important to remember that we need our people as much as they need us.

While Power is often confused with force and manipulation, it is only true power, inner power, the power to control ourselves along with the appropriate beingness that truly enlivens and inspires others. True power, therefore, is not given or taken or manipulated. True power is lived, exuded from within, demonstrated and shared. For power to be expressed outwardly, we need to consider the three important realms of actions, systems and paradigms. Actions or tasks are self-explanatory. Systems are the structures by which we operate and get things done. Paradigms are our ways of thinking and ways of being (which are also known as beingnesses) and includes our values and beliefs.

This book does not aim to be complete or all-encompassing and it intends to focus on the beingnesses required to achieve exponential power and growth. We see this as essential in acquiring power and creating results.

While other books offer invaluable insights on getting things done your way, they tend to emphasize scenarios whose applications are often limited to complicated schemes of manipulation.

True power is not Force by imposing one's will on another. Nor is it manipulation because at the heart of manipulation lies an admission that you may not be powerful enough and you therefore need to deploy some farce, force or make-believe scenario that fools others into compliance or into playing a hand less advantageous to them. While these tactics may get a result, they are much less satisfying in the end even if we win with them, because in our hearts we will always know that we only "won" because we tricked the other. While these tactics can fool others at times, they don't allow us to fool ourselves into believing that true power resides within us.

For instance, many people focus on the general techniques that usually enhance "power" (such as promoting oneself, building networks and cultivating an image). And in many cases across the board, power tends to be used synonymously with force—a tool that somehow seems to involve and necessitate persuasion, manipulation and even deception and outright warfare.

Why the effectiveness of the principles mentioned in the previous paragraph can be limited is because: (1) they foster the view that power is dependent on having a certain title, or possessing a position of influence or being in a particular situation; (2) they presume that people can remember and apply at the right moment all the hundreds and thousands of tips and techniques that grant or maximize what they call power in various situations; and (3) by confusing power with force, they leave an impression that power is somehow inherently evil—an immoral capacity that we have to exercise simply to get our way or because so much in our lives depends on it.

This book is based on an entirely different premise. It proceeds from our observations that:

1. Access to power is something all human beings have.
2. This access can be developed to extraordinary degrees by cultivating habitual ways of being rather than by memorizing routine ways of doing.
3. Power doesn't carry the negative connotations of force because it is distinct from Force.

Force is the "push" against resistance to make things happen, while power eludes resistance by using the "pull" of attraction, inspiration, alignment and partnership.

In other words, we already possess a certain amount of power and we can develop it to any degree that we desire. Furthermore, it's an ability that doesn't necessarily involve any of the negative practices that are said to go with it: practices such as persuasion, manipulation and deception.

What this book therefore describes are the fundamental bases of power—ways of being in the world that generate power as a by-product rather than as a function of personality, circumstance or strategy. Ways-of-being transcend personality, are indifferent to circumstance and ultimately underlie all strategy. They can, therefore, be applied by anyone at any time, place and situation without the usual constraint of having to act or behave in certain ways.

Having to act or behave in certain ways falls under the domain of following "laws." Because people usually relate to power as the result of acting or behaving in particular ways, books about power often talk about the "laws" of power. But laws exist only when, and because, people don't live by a common set of values. If people lived by common values, no laws would be needed. The same notion applies to so-called laws of power.

The Boss Commands while the Leader Asks

The Boss Depends on Authority while the Leader Depends on Good Will

The Boss Drives Employees while the Leader Coaches His People

WHAT IS POWER?

The Boss Generates Fear while the Leader Inspires Enthusiasm

The Boss Says "I" while the Leader Says "We."

The Boss Takes Credit while the Leader Gives the Credit Away

The Boss Uses People while the Leader Motivates People

WHAT IS LEADERSHIP?

Leadership is the ability to channel and increase energy toward a purpose and vision while being guided by values.
Bjorn Christian Martinoff

THE FORMULA FOR SUCCESS

HAVE YOU NOTICED that, at times, people know what to do but don't do what they know?

This happens more often than we would like to say. You may also have noticed that other people will get it all done even when they are already overloaded. Give the work to a busy person, the saying goes, and the work will get done.

Now we know that there aren't that many "busy" people around to fill all the personnel needs of every organization. And even if you could find a few, they might be more expensive than what your organization can afford. So you may end up with less-than-ideal talent or settle for new hires who survive rather than thrive. Now, if there was a way to transform these employees into more productive team members, wouldn't that be great? Well, the good news is it is possible—but it will take patience and skill.

First, we need to understand why people are who they are and the basic reasons why they behave how they behave. Psychology and our past have a wee bit to do with that, but it's usually not the most important or impactful in life.

In this book, we talk about some of these factors. There are barriers to overcome in life and everyone faces them. The biggest barrier is fear and we'll talk more about that in later parts of this book. Then there are stages by which leaders will need to grow. Skipping a step or being promoted too soon can cause leadership failure or lead to people just not following the "leader."

Perhaps the most important factor in achievement, success and getting things done IS…wait for it…*energy*. The level of energy we bring to the task or challenge we face is what we, as coaches, call Beingness. Maybe one out of 500 organizations will talk about Beingness; even fewer have a choice about it.

Beingness is so important that in our informal surveys, it is the number one category of factors cited by survey participants. Examples of positive Beingnesses are Alignment, Commitment, Determination, Courage and Integrity; while examples of negative Beingnesses are Anger, Impatience and Manipulation. It's the positive Beingnesses that help us succeed and overcome challenges. However, when was the last time you went into a meeting and asked yourself beforehand what Beingness you would have to bring into the meeting to cause the best possible outcome? Likely never—you never thought about it or even considered it. People generally are just not into the habit of talking about Beingness.

As coaches, we work with many highly intelligent executives and people. The vast majority of times, we notice that people actually "know" what to do in the vast majority of cases. However, it is usually not apparent to us that our Beingness, our feelings and our emotions can have a tremendous impact on the results that we can create.

So our formula for success consists of these three realms or areas:

First is DOING, with which most of us are all too familiar. Second is HAVING, which is the outcome we want to create. Third, which is too often forgotten or overlooked is BEING. BEING or BEINGNESS is what impacts EVERYTHING from start to finish.

So, what we propose is: BEING(NESS)-DOING-HAVING. These are our three realms.

Now at some point, we saw that HAVING as the outcome is like what comes after the equal (=) symbol in mathematics. This, in turn, had us wonder if there could be a mathematical relationship between BEING and DOING that would deliver HAVING.

After some trial and error, we saw that PLUS, MINUS and DIVIDE didn't work very well. What ended up making sense was multiplication. So our formula for success is now the following:

BEING x DOING = HAVING

(Our next chapter illustrates the idea above as a graph.)

The beauty is when you choose multiple BEINGnesses, they multiply each other—thereby creating EXPONENTIAL GROWTH.

Now wouldn't that be something?

Does this also work with groups or teams?

Yes it does, though the formula for teams becomes:

ALIGNMENT x BEING x DOING = HAVING

FROM REGULAR GROWTH TO EXPONENTIAL GROWTH

WHY WE LIKE to view this book as a guide to exponential growth is because when the ways of being that generate power are practiced together, their cumulative effect is exponential. The ways of being described in this book are already enormously effective when applied individually—but what they provide when they're practiced in combination, rapid succession or *en masse* is an unprecedented shift in your level of personal power and leadership that can hardly be grasped by merely reading about it. You will have to practice it to get a full grasp and understanding of the inner power that is about to be revealed to you.

The following graphics will illustrate that frequent and continuous shifts in beingness/values are inherently exponential.

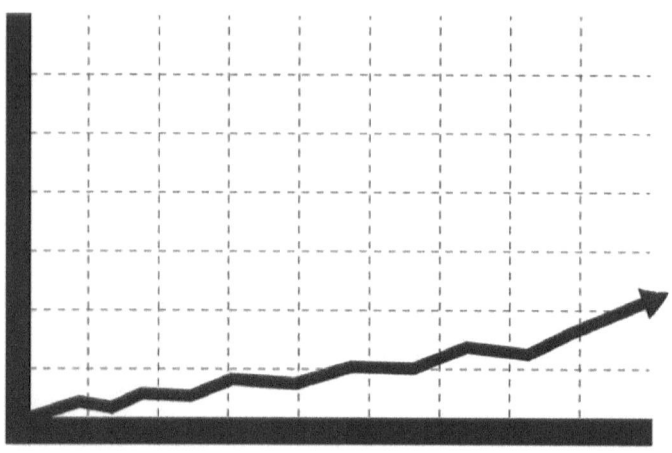

GRAPHIC 1.0: NORMAL GROWTH

This is roughly what we would expect to see in normal growth: a steady incline with some minor ups and downs.

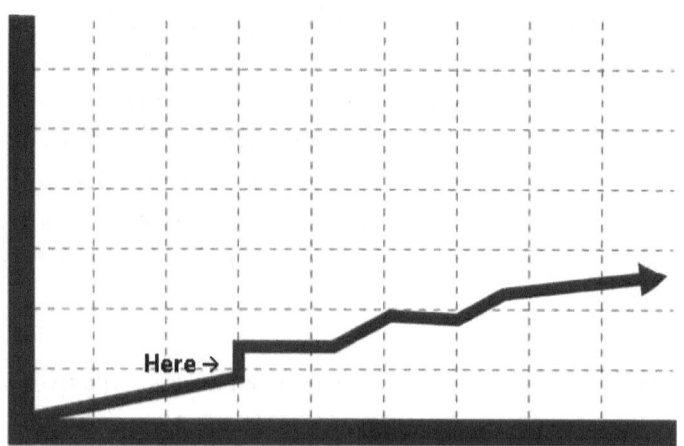

GRAPHIC 2.0: GROWTH THROUGH UPGRADED SKILLS

There is a small but nearly immediate impact from upgraded skills, but when observed further, this doesn't translate into a trajectory with a steeper angle. It does, however, translate into continued normal growth at a slightly higher level.

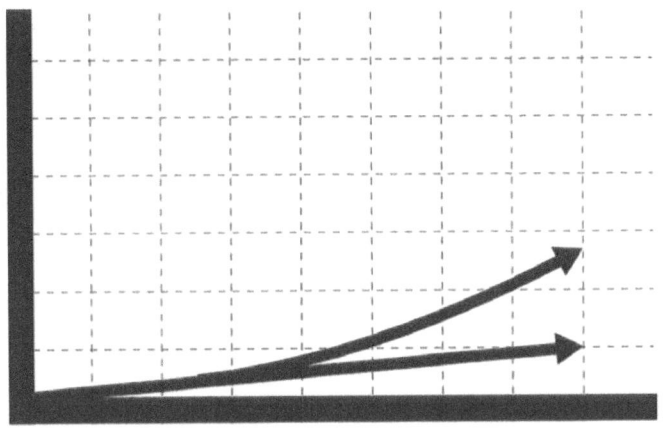

GRAPHIC 3.0: GROWTH
AFTER LIFE-CHANGING IMPACT

Here the angle or trajectory has taken on a new direction which, over time, will make a major difference. While the impact may occur as small in the beginning, over time it becomes greater and greater compared with the original "normal" growth trajectory in Graphic 1.0 and becomes quite large over time.

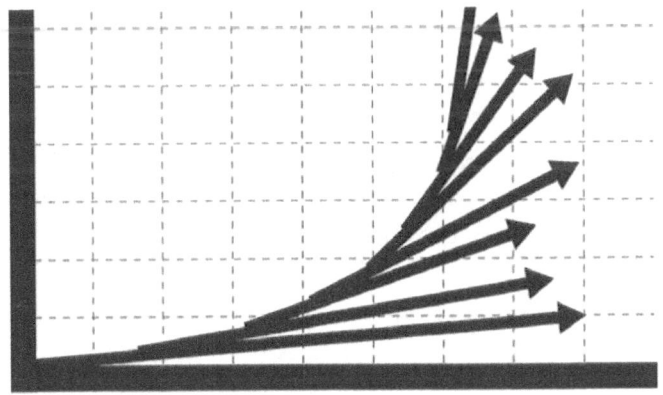

GRAPHIC 4.0: EXPONENTIAL
POWER AND GROWTH AS A RESULT
OF REPEATED LIFE CHANGES IN BEING

What is shown in Graphic 4.0 is the impact on the growth of the learner after frequently repeated life-changing shifts in beingness.

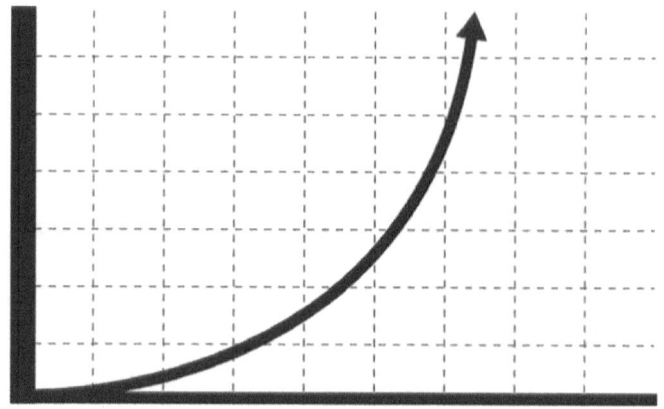

GRAPHIC 5.0: EXPONENTIAL GROWTH MEANS RADICAL RESULTS

In Graphic 5.0, we have cleaned up the curve in Graphic 4.0. It is now more visible how exponential growth can be made accessible to individuals. However, this is not just for individuals—it is also possible for teams and entire organizations.

Is exponential growth unusual? Not in nature. In nature, everything grows exponentially. Plants grow exponentially. What is unusual is that we think we can only grow at 4, 5, 6 or 10 percent per year.

While we have attempted to present these ideas in straightforward language, this content can be viewed as a highly advanced conversation.

Each chapter in this book presents an opportunity to change your life in a significant way that can empower you dramatically. When combined, these teachings will help you grow exponentially as you translate each chapter from knowledge into action. Because it needs to be put into action, we say knowledge is worthless. Or to be more precise: knowledge that isn't being used is worthless. Knowledge that is put into action becomes highly valuable.

So take caution. The knowledge you gain here by itself will make no difference. It will, however, make a BIG difference once you apply the knowledge that you will gain from this book. The difference the application of this knowledge will make is exponential.

True power is accessible to all people independent of their background, levels of education and motivation— whether they be executives who have likely already read other sources on power and leadership or younger people who may never have previously read anything on the subject.

Whatever your background or your motivation may be in reading or examining this book, it is designed to provide you with access to more—much more—access to your inner power, AND, the ability to live this new power, making it an experience that will leave you touched, moved and inspired.

May you use this power to become the master of your own destiny—and may you use the influence you subsequently generate wisely and for the good of all humanity!

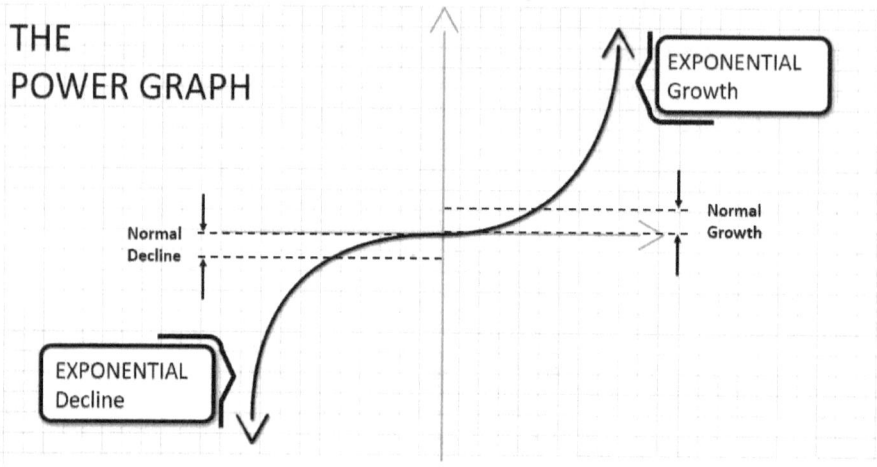

GROWTH ONLY HAPPENS OUTSIDE OF THE COMFORT ZONE

> *If you don't frequently venture outside your comfort zone, you are not growing. And when you are not growing, you are not maximizing your life. The same goes for your people.*
> **Bjorn Christian Martinoff**

MEASURING GROWTH ON THE POWER SCALE

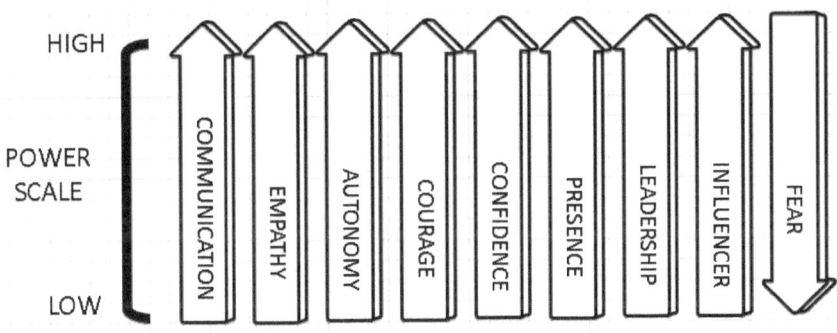

WHEN WE GO up the power scale, all the beingnesses we need are increasing and growing. The only one that is decreasing is fear.

THE 3.5 STAGES OF GROWTH

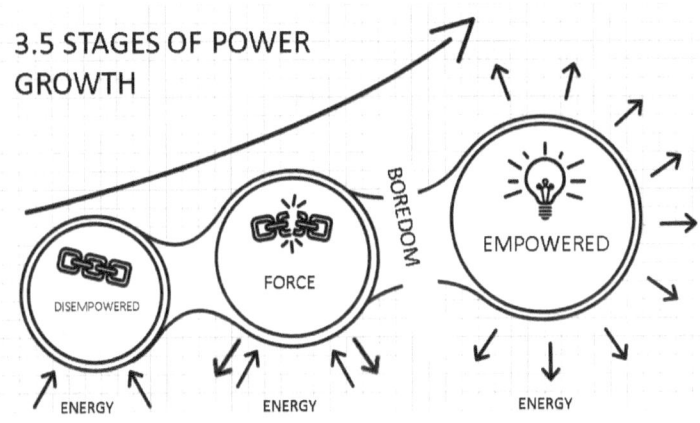

POWER DOESN'T HAVE an on-and-off switch unless you are talking about the power coming from your outlet. Power comes to us in stages depending on what stage we find ourselves at any moment. We all go through these stages. There is no escaping it.

The stages distinguish themselves through energy. Popular myth says that there is positive energy and negative energy. Yet, we find that energy is neither inherently positive nor negative. However, it can be perceived that way. It can be perceived as positive or negative because energy can have direction. Direction means that energy either comes to us or flows away from us to have an impact. If it flows away from us, it lowers our energy—which means we perceive it as negative. When energy flows toward us, it raises our energy—which means we perceive it as positive.

In my book *Develop Exponential Power: Stop Chasing It and Let It Chase You*, I showed the difference between Power and Force where Power results in the increase in energy of people while Force results in the decrease in energy.

With regard to Power, there are stages through which our personal inner and external power evolves. All of them are distinguished by the direction of energy.

STAGE 1.0: DIS-EMPOWERED

In the first stage which we call Dis-Empowered, we have not yet found our own power and confidence. This is made visible by a victim mentality. Rather than creating our own destiny, we are at the mercy of others, our life and our circumstances. Because of this lack of energy, people in this stage can be highly self-centered—even selfish. They are leaching energy from others, which is demonstrated by the arrows pointing towards them. They are low on power or energy and they therefore get it from others. In this stage, fear is high.

STAGE 2.0: FORCE

To get out from Dis-Empowerment, we often discover that we can do this by forcing ourselves to do things we are otherwise too afraid to do, too stressed out to tackle, normally lack the courage to attack or simply feel too weak to address. In this stage, we force ourselves out of our usual mode and do things we normally wouldn't do. This is often preceded by feeling angry, upset, weak or hopeless in the Dis-Empowered stage.

This stage can help us move up the self-empowerment ladder, but people can find themselves trying to "support" others by forcing them as well. This can have a negative impact on others and actually reduces their energy.

People applying force are usually unaware of their negative impact on others and often believe that force is the only way to get things going.

In this stage, energy is stronger than in the Dis-Empowered stage, but it isn't stable and it tends to fluctuate between giving and receiving energy. People in this stage can sometimes share their energy with others and sometimes they can act like sponges sucking energy from others. That is why in the graphic you see the arrows or vectors going in opposite directions. This stage is where you can find the so-called "alpha" leaders. Alpha leaders sometimes increase the energy of those around them and sometimes decrease the energy of those around them. They are not yet stable in their source of energy. Their energy fluctuates and their impact can vary between Alpha and Alpha-Hole—the latter meaning a black hole that sucks the energy out of others. The term Alpha-hole is not to be confused with the popular street term of A--Hole.

To move from the stage of Dis-Empowerment to the stage of Force, we need to increase our energy. And

to move ourselves from the stage of Force to the next stage, we need to increase our energy again. However, any attempt to get people in line through force just lowers their energy; they will react with even stronger force or, worse, go back into Dis-Empowerment.
In Stage 2.0, fear is lessened by the use of control. Control is a form of force and lowers energy in those being controlled.

STAGE 2.5: BOREDOM

There is a stage between force and empowerment which we call the stage of boredom. In this stage, energy doesn't flow in either direction. It's just there. Fear has almost disappeared in this stage. If we keep empowering people at this stage, they will move on to the next stage.

STAGE 3.0: EMPOWERED AND EMPOWERING

Stage 3.0 distinguishes itself by the outflow of power and energy and therefore is a level of power even higher than an Alpha leader's. One might say that the Alpha leader does not yet possess true power as their energy and power can fluctuate greatly depending on many things and circumstances. In Stage 3.0, we encounter truly powerful and energetic people. We can tell by how much power, energy and empowerment flows from them.

Fear has virtually disappeared in this stage. Human beings often arrive here either by being empowered or by being courage junkies who have continually looked for new ways of experiencing the thrill of courage. Many chief executive officers are in this space of courage, yet quite a number can also just be in the earlier stages.

Everyone surrounding a Stage 3.0 person experiences the great energy they exude. They are generating enough energy to share it with others, nurture others, develop others and empower others.

This is why there's a saying that you can tell true masters not by their own achievements but by the achievements and mastery of those they developed.

If you find yourself in the lower stages, don't make yourself wrong or blame yourself. Find ways to empower yourself instead. There are many ways of doing this such as attending seminars, learning meditation, reading books, finding a coach, elevating your spirituality, finding a church that inspires and motivates you, etc. There are self-empowerment communities out there and once you gain access by participating in their learning events, they will often share with you what helped them empower themselves. Don't worry about looking bad—looking bad is one of those concerns that will stop you dead in your tracks. So ignore it and go ahead.

THE HIGHEST BARRIERS TO INDIVIDUAL GROWTH

IT'S TIME TO talk about the enemies and thieves that are in the way of our potential as professionals and as human beings. They are serious enemies and they will steal from us anything they can. They do this with a sincere accomplice. This accomplice is you. They do it by pretending to be your friends. They aren't your friends as we will demonstrate in a moment. Yet for most of your life—if not for your entire life—they may have deceived you into thinking of them as friends.

Where are these thieves? Where are these enemies? They are right here beside you. You might even consider that they are inside you. Now as you read these lines, you may have already gotten signals of wanting to stop reading this. Yes, this is your first enemy in action. It will try and stop you through feelings of anxiety, stress and uneasiness. Anxiety and stress are just fancy modern names for this enemy. We have a much less fancy name for it.

We call it FEAR. Fear in all its versions will rear its ugly head in many seemingly helpful disguises. It may call itself hesitation, reluctance, shyness or timidity. No matter what form or shape it takes, its goal is to stop you. Even if it shows up to make you feel it's here to protect you, fear is always there to stop you. What's there to protect you is reality and a good sense of reality will protect you. Why fear looks like a protector is because you are confusing it with reality.

The next thief or enemy is called FORCE. Force also wants to come across as your friend. It tends to disguise itself as POWER. But Force doesn't equal Power even though the world at large is confused between these two. The world largely tends to think of these as equals. Yet they are not. Far from being equal, Force and Power are opposites. Force decreases energy while Power increases energy. Imagine someone forcing you to do something. Will you be inspired? No. Of course not. Hardly anyone is inspired, energized or enthused when being forced to do something. In our informal surveys, 99 percent of the people we asked are not enthused and report that their energy goes down when they're forced. True Power doesn't decrease energy; it increases it. To learn more about Power and Force, I highly encourage you to read my book *Develop Exponential Power: Stop Chasing It and Let It Chase You*.

The third enemy is OVER-CONFIDENCE. Over-confidence, also known as arrogance, disguises itself as your friend by referring to itself as certainty. Certainty can bring with it a certain level of confidence. When you are in fear, certainty and arrogance may seem like a much better frame of mind than fear. However, the problem with over-confidence is that it will seem as if we've already mastered everything we need to know. But we don't. We don't know everything. We will never know everything as the knowledge out there is just too vast. Over-confidence is a trap disguised as certainty. Don't fall for it. Every time you think you already know it all, you are being fooled and trapped by arrogance. With over-confidence and arrogance, learning stops. With real certainty, we know where we are and where we are not—and that keeps the doors open to new learning. The next thing is to keep on learning.

The last enemy is OLD AGE. This is an enemy we can only overcome temporarily. Much has been written about it already and so we won't say much about it here.

In life, we need to learn to recognize and overcome these enemies (except the last). If we don't, they will steal our possibilities, our opportunities and our potential.

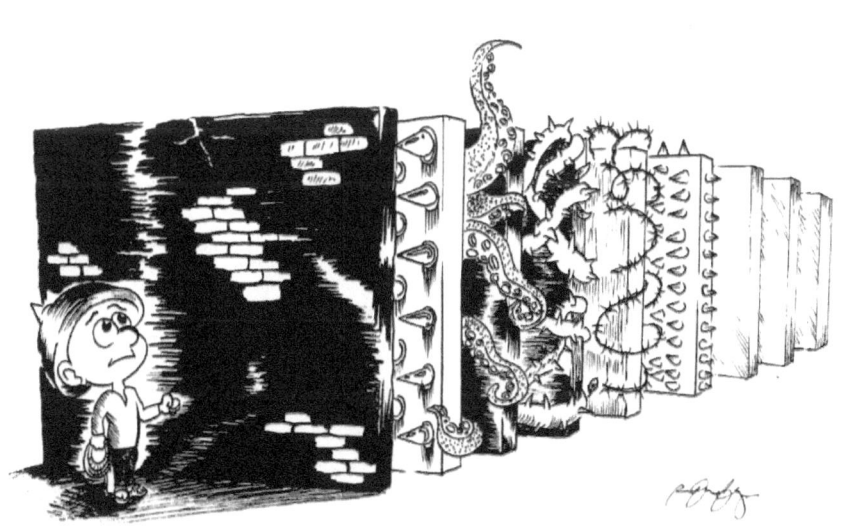

WHAT SLOWS DOWN YOUR LEADERSHIP TEAM

IT WOULD BE easy to assume that team-building should be the same whether at a supervisory level, managerial level or at a leadership team level. This is not the case, however. Executive teams tend to be older, wiser, highly intelligent and more confident, but often less fit, more easily bored, more challenging, more critical and have much higher expectations. Such teams require facilitators with much higher levels of experience, matching levels of confidence, broader exposure and a sure-footedness that has to be powerful yet demonstrates great humility at the same time.

There are specifics things to watch out for that can slow down your executive team, and your facilitator should be able to detect these beforehand through observation, interviews or focus group discussions.

The following lists things that can slow your leadership team down, lowering their energy, effectiveness and results.

1. **Misalignment.** When team members push in differing directions, much momentum is lost immediately and much time is spent arguing over

the direction to take. In our experience, we have seen an energy differential of as much as 90 percent. Given these tremendous losses in energy and momentum, one may wonder why there are teams and organizations that don't take the time to align themselves. Time itself is often the reason or the excuse. When you realize, however, how much *more* time is lost by misalignment, the actual time spent aligning is more than worth it.

2. **Distrust.** It is amazing how little trust there often is amongst leadership team members. Often this is caused by seeing each other from what Harvard Business School would call a mechanistic perspective of perceiving each other like parts of a machine. We tend to see machines as having predictable outcomes. This hardly ever will be the case in leadership teams as leadership teams tend to venture out into the unknown, whether the unknown is a new level of performance, a new market or a new product.

3. **The Past.** Many times, teams are slowed down by something that happened in the past. It might be a prior disagreement, argument or misalignment. These feelings can carry forward into the future and can be quite disabling for even the most outstanding individuals.

4. **Low Spirits.** The spirit of the team can be extremely impactful on the performance of the team. Their level of performance will subsequently have an impact on their overall results.

5. **Just Doing the Job.** Most often found in uninspired and mechanistic organizational cultures as well as in command-and-control leadership scenarios (which we discuss later), "just doing the job" means leaving your brain at the door. Unfortunately, no brain, no gain.

6. **Our Culture is Better than Yours.** Many multinational teams or team members are afflicted by this and only few consultants know how to address this. This can cause a rift among the different nationalities on the team as no one wants to have the "wrong" culture and everyone wants to have the "right" culture. This can also occur when you are in transition from an "old" culture to a "new" culture or from a traditional or hierarchical culture to a more modern way of relating and working together.

7. **No Trust or Low Trust.** Without courage there is no authenticity, and without authenticity, there is no trust. Without trust, there is no teamwork. Without teamwork, there is no team. Without the team, there are only silos. When there are only silos, it's everyone for themselves.

8. **Low Confidence.** The role of an executive team is to lead where no one has gone before and have others follow. No one is going to follow a low confidence leader, much less a low confidence leadership team.

9. **No Authenticity of Limited Authenticity.** Authenticity is when what we say and what we mean are the same. Without authenticity, the lips might be moving, words might be spoken, but NOTHING is being said. It's a complete waste of time. Imagine an entire team pretending to communicate. The only place that team is going fast is NOWHERE.

10. **Overdrawn Emotional Bank Accounts.** Let's face it: mistakes will be made. It's how your

team handles mistakes that matters. There is the immature way to handle it which is to counter and to attack. There is the "hurt" way to handle it which is to refuse to forgive. There is the more mature way to handle it which is to be authentic, to be real about what worked and what didn't work, to learn from it, to look at what could have been done differently, to move on, to right what was wrong and to succeed. There's no other way to do it.

11. **Low or No Courage.** It takes courage to be authentic. So, courage and authenticity are emotional key performance indicators that allow us to predict where a team is going and how fast it's getting there.

12. **Lack of Integrity.** Integrity is more than what you think it is. It doesn't just mean that there are no lies. Integrity means that we keep our word and when we give our word it is like gold. There is integrity with time, integrity with our promises, integrity with our results and integrity with the way we do things. Integrity means we operate at the highest level anyone could expect us to operate.

13. **High Fear.** High fear leads to low courage or no courage and no confidence. No confidence means no leadership. When we cannot lead ourselves, others won't follow us.

14. **Followers Not Leaders.** Followers may boost your ego, but leaders will boost your results. Imagine a team of leaders and not just a team of followers. Yes, it's harder to lead leaders no doubt,

but the rewards are tremendous. The truth is that not everyone is cut out to lead leaders.

15. **Operating in Silos.** It's a great tragedy when you have departments competing with each other rather than with the competition. Guess who pays the price?

16. **Underutilized and or Repressed Potential.** Your facilitator needs to know how to unleash your team's potential. Sadly there are only few that do. Most people we interview report that, on average, only 80 percent of their potential is being utilized by their company.

17. **Command-and-Control Leadership.** Command-and-control leadership leads to limited engagement, limited involvement, blind obedience, low creativity and slow growth. Such leadership

can still be found in more traditional or family-run operations. This won't attract any great talent as the leader always gets all the credit.

18. **Lack of Purpose.** Many leaders, consultants and facilitators are confused between purpose and mission. By definition, a mission is merely

a description of what you do—which is hardly inspiring. Develop a purpose instead. Develop something that inspires the heart and that gets each and every one of your team members out of bed in the morning. When they snooze, you lose.

The above are just some of the things that may hold your top team back, but they're certainly not all. It takes someone with extensive experience in working at executive level coaching and developing to address such issues. Go for the interventions you need and unleash your team so you can say goodbye to low growth and low performance and say hi to paradigm shifts, breakthroughs and miracles.

BREAKDOWN BEFORE BREAKTHROUGH

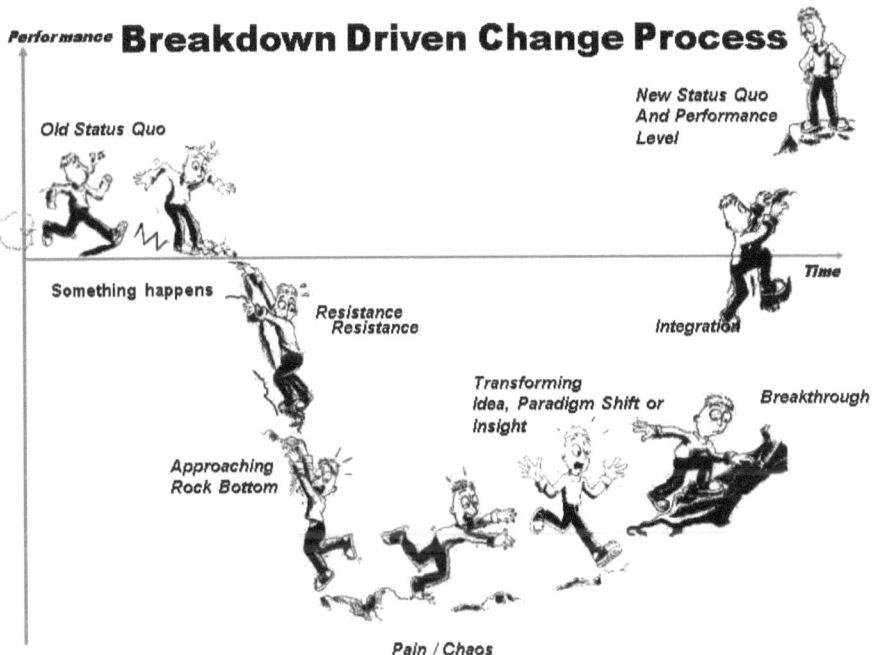

This is the usual way breakdowns and breakthroughs occur without external intervention.

BEFORE BREAKTHROUGHS HAPPEN, there is usually a breakdown. This could be in the shape or form of a mistake, a mishap, a failure or an accident.
Such a breakdown can make someone really think and contemplate, and this is how the breakthrough occurs. Once the learning from the breakdown is applied and implemented, a new and improved level of

performance will become apparent.

The important part is in how we treat the breakdown. IT IS IMPERATIVE to not go into blaming, but to focus on finding the facts and to ask what could have been done differently, how the breakdown could have been prevented or what can be learned to help us improve.

THE EVOLUTIONARY STAGES IN DEVELOPING LEADERS

LEADERS AREN'T NECESSARILY born—they're forged through the fires of hardship, trial and tribulation. Anyone can become a leader with enough patience and persistence. In this section, we'll go through the stages involved in cultivating leadership.

1. **Leading the Self.** Before we can lead anyone else, we need to be able to lead ourselves. In our experience, the vast majority of "leaders" fail because they've ignored, overlooked or sidestepped this vastly crucial stage of development.

   On the most practical level, learning how to lead ourselves means giving ourselves the opportunity to discover, explore and overcome the various kinds of resistance that arise when one is leading another. If we don't know what the obstacles to leadership in the personal domain are—if we've never encountered them, attempted to engage with them and never surmounted them—how can we expect to be leaders in the professional domain? We wouldn't have the mastery, let alone the credibility.

   The good news, learning how to lead ourselves is something we can start at *any* time. It's regrettably not taught in schools, but perhaps that will change one day. Until that day comes, it's a task we'll have to undertake by ourselves. This includes being able to overcome and surmount challenging or even frightening situations. As leaders, we constantly need to go beyond our comfort zone and inspire our people to do the same. So practice early on in your career to leave your comfort zone. It's a muscle that gets built with practice. Every time you do something new, uncomfortable or scary, the more your courage "muscle" will grow. There is no switch that can turn on your courage permanently other than building that muscle.

2. **Leading Followers.** Once we have succeeded in leading ourselves, we can undertake the challenge of leading followers—that is, individuals whose level

of authority or responsibility in an organization is below ours. At this level of leadership, what's critical is being able to "walk our talk" (if we've done the work of leading ourselves, walking our talk should be a walk in the park, pun not intended). It's important to note that people always do what a leader does rather than do what the leader says. That is, people unconsciously model their behavior on the leader's *behavior* rather than the leader's *instructions*. So, if a leader insists on a company policy of punctuality, but is consistently late for his or her meetings, you can imagine the extent to which that policy is going to be followed by the company's employees.

3. **Leading Peers.** Once we have succeeded in leading followers, the next and even more challenging stage is leading peers—that is, individuals whose level of authority or responsibility in an organization equals ours. This equality means that we cannot use our position to influence a peer in the same way that we would be able to use our position to influence a follower. Hence, leading peers requires an entirely different set of skills or an entirely different level of mastery of the same set of skills—skills such as generating alignment, cultivating empathy, encouraging flexibility, having fun, listening well and creating inspiration.

4. **Leading Leaders.** Once we have succeeded in leading followers, the next stage is leading leaders—that is, individuals whose level of authority or responsibility in an organization exceeds ours, or, individuals who belong to a different organization (or a different part of an organization) altogether. Although it sounds like a skill that we'll rarely, if

ever, get to practice, leading leaders happens far more often than we think.

For example, sales people embody this type of leadership when they influence independent decision-makers to finalize a purchase. Subordinates also embody this type of leadership when they influence executives at higher levels. If you find yourself hesitating as you're reading this because what we're describing doesn't sound like leadership, we'll quote Unilever Chief Executive Officer Paul Polman's definition of leadership. As he puts it: "My definition of leadership is very simple: if you positively influence someone, you are a leader."

In short, leading leaders is about possessing the ways of being and the skills necessary to influence leadership at levels higher than one's own. And this is vitally important, because the highest levels of leaders—global leaders who are the heads of huge multinational firms and world leaders who are the heads of states—*need* the guidance, knowledge and support of subordinates who are aligned with the same vision and purpose and guided by the same values *but* are *the* masters in their own domain of expertise. Leaders at the highest level simply do not and cannot know every aspect of the organization and its workings. Hence, for such leaders to succeed, they paradoxically need "followers" who can lead them!

EXPONENTIAL BREAKTHROUGH LEADERSHIP

IN OUR PREFACE to this book, we spoke of the distinction between Power and Force. To briefly review what we said then, Power gives people a choice, freedom and self-respect and ultimately unleashes their energy. Force, on the other hand, takes away people's choice, freedom and self-respect and ultimately drains their energy.

In our preface, we also mentioned how Power is the mark of true Leadership, while Force is a symptom of mere Management. The frightening thing is that the majority of the world's organizations are being run by Managers who employ Force—and thereby drain energy—rather than by Leaders who cultivate Power—and thereby unleash energy. This is a highly undesirable and unsustainable state of affairs given that, more than ever, organizations around the world at every level need as much energy as they can generate to address the pressing and urgent issues confronting our businesses, our industries, our families, our communities, our societies and our countries.

In other words, the presence of Force rather than Power and the predominance of Management over Leadership is a concern that affects us both in the for-profit sector and the non-profit sector.

In this section of the book, we're going to more closely examine what genuine Leadership is, and we're going to do this with an intention to eventually replace the culture of Force and Management that's currently in place with a culture of Power and Leadership. We'll begin by examining what we refer to as Exponential Breakthrough Leadership.

The concept of Exponential Breakthrough Leadership began with the notion of transformational leadership that was pioneered by presidential biographer and leadership expert James MacGregor Burns. This notion is premised, in turn, on the observation that leaders can be divided into four categories: (1) those who don't actually lead; (2) those who can lead followers; (3) those who can lead peers; and (4) those who can lead leaders.

Exponential Breakthrough Leadership belongs to the fourth category of leaders leading leaders. At this level of leadership, organizations are able to attain exponentially higher levels of performance as well as breakthrough results. What are the characteristics of leaders who can lead leaders? Very briefly:

- They forge new perspectives and new paradigms.
- They can harness the strength of their vision and their personality.
- They can inspire those around them to align with mutually chosen directions, goals and ways of working.
- They enjoy the company of their fellows and find work just as fun and rewarding as play.
- They have the trust, respect and admiration of their

teams.
- ☐ They speak last in order to give everyone the opportunity to have a voice

To help make the notion of Exponential Breakthrough Leadership more accessible and understandable, we've broken it down into the following components:

1. **Ongoing Transformation.** Exponential Breakthrough Leaders not only challenge themselves to grow continuously, shift their paradigms, think "outside of the box" and expand— but they challenge the rest of their team as well. And they do this from a space of infectious enthusiasm, excitement and passion so that their team members don't feel like they "have" to do it, but rather they *want* to do it.

2. **Authentic Communication.** Exponential Breakthrough Leaders create avenues for authentic communication where ideas, information, feedback and even emotions can be shared freely without judgment or criticism. They foster an environment where team members feel safe in expressing themselves candidly and with the assurance that they will be heard and understood.

3. **Intrinsic Motivation.** Exponential Breakthrough Leaders foster alignment with their organization's purpose, vision and values and then *embody* rather than merely express the organization's purpose, vision and values. By acting as role models, they cultivate internal rather than external motivation amongst their team members. Their teams are engaged, empowered and inspired to go beyond their expected targets.

4. **Genuine Concern.** Exponential Breakthrough Leaders continuously provide their team members with encouragement, recognition, and support. They constantly look for ways of developing, empowering and nurturing their teams and do so with a genuine concern that goes beyond the demands of the workplace.

> ### THE POWER OF GENUINE CONCERN
>
> My dear friend Yehuda Berg once told me of how his father's teacher, Ray Brandwein, inspired a prominent mayor to quit smoking. Mr. Brandwein never judged the mayor for his smoking habit—he didn't even speak to the mayor about the dangers of smoking let alone ask him to quit. However, the mayor felt so much care and concern coming from Mr. Brandwein's regard that it was enough to *make* him quit smoking.
>
> What I love about this story is how it demonstrates the power of genuine concern. People who indulge in vices do so because, on some subconscious level, they don't think of themselves as worthy of deep care and concern. So when they experience real and authentic regard from someone else, it opens up the possibility that they *are* worth caring for and this gives them a new way of relating to themselves. And without any persuasion or force, they

> naturally begin to drop the vice.
>
> The same principle applies to true leadership. True leadership doesn't need to resort to giving advice or lectures. Instead, they simply assure people that they are worthy of genuine concern, permit them to go through their process and give them the time and space to change at their own pace. As I often like to say, when an egg is broken open from the outside, life ends. But when the egg is broken open from the inside, life begins. Genuine leadership is about helping people break their eggs *from the inside—* where it truly matters.

5. **Future-Based Languaging.** Although Exponential Breakthrough Leaders keep their feet planted squarely in the present, they keep their eyes on the future, focusing on what needs to be accomplished to achieve the organization's objectives without indulging in complaints or protests about the challenges of the present.

Now, Exponential Breakthrough Leaders are also characterized by particular ways of being—all of which are described in my first book *Develop Exponential Power: Stop Chasing It and Let It Chase You* (this is a very important book and one we highly recommend you read!). Some ways of being mentioned in that book are so important that we'll briefly summarize them here:

1. **Integrity.** Integrity is an essential quality of Exponential Breakthrough Leaders. The most powerful definition of integrity we've encountered was developed by Erhard Seminars Training Founder Werner Erhard who defined it as "honoring one's word" by "doing what you said you would do and by the time you said you would do it." Furthermore, if you aren't able to do what you said you would do and by the time you said you would do it, you would acknowledge your breakdown with the people who were impacted, ask them how you can address the impact and then make a new promise. He also says that integrity is doing things the best way they can be expected to be done or better! While this sounds simple enough, practicing integrity in this way is *enormously* challenging and demands an elevated level of continued personal commitment.

2. **Alignment.** The ability to create alignment is a crucial skill required of Exponential Breakthrough Leaders. Even if an organization has a clearly and powerfully defined purpose, vision and set of values, it will still fail to generate breakthrough—or even passable—results if its members are interpreting its purpose, vision and values in divergent or contradictory ways (whether consciously or unconsciously). Only leaders who can create true alignment within their groups can produce the kind of breakthrough results that are generated when every member of a team is working towards the same outcome. Again, this sounds simple enough in theory but is exceedingly difficult to master in practice. That's why purpose, vision and values are easily in alignment when they were created together. We do this in our workshops when helping

executive teams unleash their purpose, vision and values in a process of co-creation.

3. **Humility.** Exponential Breakthrough Leaders possess the humility and the maturity needed to recognize that other people in their team may be more appropriate in leading particular initiatives or projects given their unique competencies and skills. This means that Exponential Breakthrough Leaders are comfortable with sharing leadership and are unconcerned about positions and titles. They implicitly recognize that they can share their power without having their own power being diminished in any way.

A WORD ON COMMAND-AND-CONTROL LEADERSHIP

When we're trying to understand what something is, it's often very helpful to also understand what it's not. Hence, in this section on Exponential Breakthrough Leadership, we'll also briefly examine its opposite—which we refer to as Command-and-Control Leadership and which we've referred to in earlier sections of this book.

Command-and-Control Leadership is characterized by what Harvard University refers to as "mechanistic cultures." In such organizations, employees are thought of as cogs in a well-oiled machine that are merely expected to execute commands issued from on high. In such cultures, employees are not expected to think because their task is to simply do what they're told when they're told. The limitations of such a corporate culture are glaringly obvious: there is no initiative, no ownership, no choice and no inspiration and the organization loses out on the brilliance, creativity and engagement of practically its entire workforce.

It's also the kind of organization that, to introduce concepts we'll discuss later, requires rules to govern its employees' behavior and Managers to enforce those rules.

Organizations run by Exponential Breakthrough Leaders, on the other hand, simply rely on values to inspire their employees' behavior and have Leaders that embody those values.

WOMEN AND EXPONENTIAL LEADERSHIP

There was a story that circulated on the Internet once about how former United States President Barack Obama took First Lady Michelle Obama out to dinner. At the restaurant, they discovered that the owner was a former boyfriend of the First Lady's. The First Couple was treated to a lovely evening which they very much enjoyed. After they had left, the President turned to the First Lady and asked if she weren't glad that she had ended up with him given that she would have ended up as the wife of a restaurant owner otherwise. The First Lady responded by saying that if she had married her ex, *he* would have ended up being the president of the United States!

Whether or not it's true, the story points to a certain, often overlooked truth, which is that women possess a natural, nurturing and quiet leadership style of their own. They also develop leadership skills much earlier than men do. If you watch little boys play, they prefer rough-and-tumble games like Cops versus Robbers—games that involve combat, domination and weaponry. If you watch little girls play, they prefer relational games like tea parties—games that involve communication, empathy and understanding. In other words, boys gravitate towards Force very early on while girls gravitate towards Power.

If anything, this edge that women possess has only become sharper over the centuries as they've been suppressed by men, by religion, by society and by culture. Repeatedly demonized, persecuted and oppressed—often at the hands of their own fathers, husbands and sons—women have learned to channel and express their Power in unobtrusive ways, learning how to influence and inspire from the shadows and the sidelines without authority or recognition. Women have learned how to wield their Power from positions of disadvantage and within the limited spheres of raising their children and supporting their husbands. As the saying goes, "Behind every great man, there's a great woman." (Or as we've heard it revised, "Behind every great man, there's a woman wishing he'd get the hell out of her way.")

Of course, we're not saying that all women possess this Power or can express it. Neither are we saying that men don't possess this Power or can't develop it. All we're saying is that women have a natural gift for bringing out the best in people and have a natural capacity for a style of leadership that's remarkably like Exponential Breakthrough Leadership. The sooner we recognize this, the better, because as we've mentioned earlier, organizations around the world at every level are in desperate need of Exponential Breakthrough Leaders—*yet keep ignoring the women*.

We urgently need to recognize the leadership gifts that women naturally possess. First, we desperately need those gifts. In a world driven apart by conflict, terrorism and war, we need leaders whose first instinct is *not* to shoot the enemy at the first sign of provocation. We need leaders who are, quite literally, ready to sit down to tea and *talk*. Second, for as long as we don't recognize the value of women's leadership style, they will continue to be forced to develop the more Forceful leadership style of men—a style which is not only unnatural to women but is also becoming increasingly inappropriate in the world today.

As William Golding once said, "I think women are foolish to pretend they are equal to men, they are far superior and always have been."

VECTORING ENERGY ADDED TO FORMULA = TEAM SUCCESS FORMULA

> *Just as your car runs more smoothly and requires less energy to go faster and farther when the wheels are in perfect alignment, you and your team perform better when your thoughts, feelings, emotions, goals, actions and values are in alignment with where you're heading.*
> **Bjorn Christian Martinoff**

IN OUR EXPERIENCE working with different companies from all over the world—partnering with individual executives of small companies, large companies, struggling companies, Fortune 100 companies, or even the world's largest company—we've found that one of the biggest things that gets in the way of their success is the absence of alignment. The absence of alignment is one of the greatest detractors from power being applied toward the desired goal.

Alignment is critical in any organization because without broad-based agreement on goals, strategies, and other critical areas, organizations can literally spend a LOT of energy without getting anywhere.

Why?

Well, imagine sitting on a boat with two people rowing: one person is rowing in one direction and the other person is rowing in the opposite direction. If they're both putting in the same amount of energy, they'll just end up canceling each other's efforts and the boat won't move from its location. Or, if one person is putting in more energy than the other, the boat will move in his or her direction, but at a much slower pace than they should be getting with the amount of effort they're exerting.

Now imagine this scenario replicated hundreds of times over in the average-sized organization. In the absence of alignment, there's either no progress at all, or the progress is severely hindered, or it might be severely limited AND going in a different direction than intended.

With alignment, on the other hand, all the individual energies add up and result in a huge amount of momentum. So in cases where a company has clearly established its purpose, its goals, its values and its strategies—and theoretically they're sound—but the company isn't going anywhere, one fruitful area to examine is whether the organization has worked on getting broad-based consensus for its plans.

To illustrate our point, there was one particular company in Asia that has just been warned by its client in the United States that they were at risk of losing their $11,000,000 account. Let's spell that out: that's *eleven million dollars*. At the moment we learned about this, the business unit ranked last among its network of peers. The client had given it just *two months* to turn the situation around. If not, the client would pull out. When we started our engagement with the company, we quickly realized that even just in terms of handling the crisis, there was *no* alignment among the top management team. The energies of the leaders were dispersed, their ideas mixed and unclear and the way forward was vague and uncharted. Something was left to be discovered which would make a difference but none of the leaders could say what it was.

After launching an initial set of diagnostic tools, one of the first things we did with the management team was to help them find alignment and create, in partnership with them, a common purpose, vision and set of core values.

This wasn't the only intervention we applied, but creating alignment on this broad level provided the foundation for all the other work we needed to do with the organization. Without alignment in terms of the direction we were heading, everything else would have fallen on deaf ears. Once alignment was in place, the team went on to become the number *two* performer in their network and the number *one* performer in their country—*in less than two months*. And none of this would have been possible without an initial alignment of the individual forces.

>
> *Misaligned or even opposing energies and forces are some of the greatest waste and missed opportunities you'll find in organizations.*
> **Bjorn Christian Martinoff**
>

To further demonstrate this, as well as the concept of vector dynamics in leadership, let's look at the following graphics:

GRAPHIC 1:

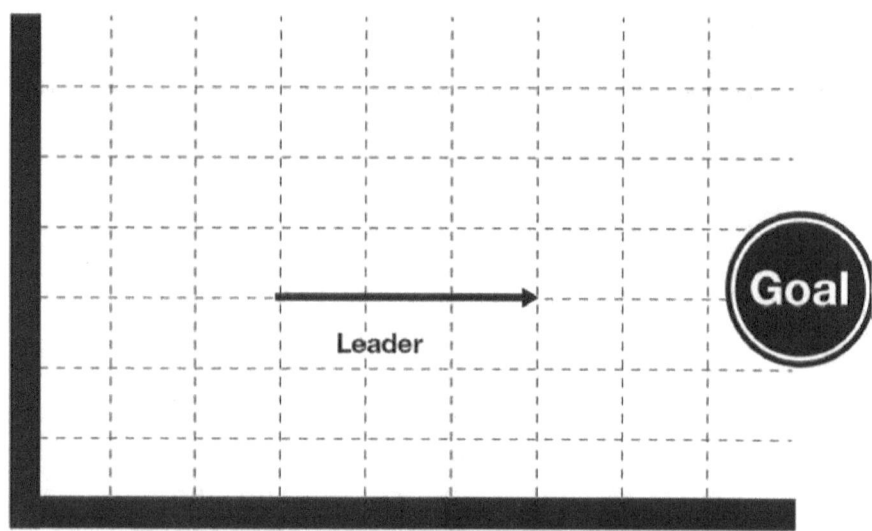

Graphic 1 represents the vector dynamics of a single leader pushing in the direction of her goals or vision. She is a strong leader. By definition though, you aren't a leader if you're doing it alone, so let's introduce some team members.

GRAPHIC 2:

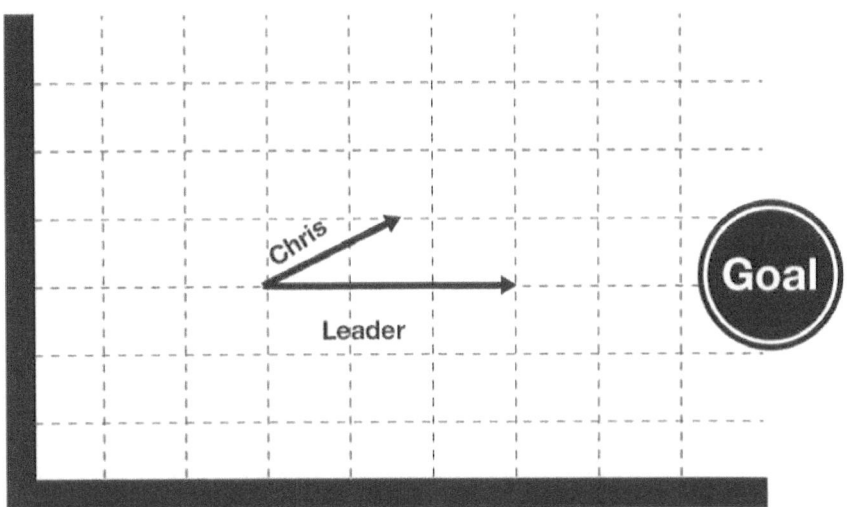

In Graphic 2, we get Chris as a member of the team. Chris is a professional and appears to be a good team player. Upon further inspection, however, we notice that Chris has an agenda of his own that's not fully aligned with the leader. We realize this must have an impact on their combined performance. The question is how much—and we'll see that in the following graphics. In the meantime let's add a few more team members.

GRAPHIC 3:

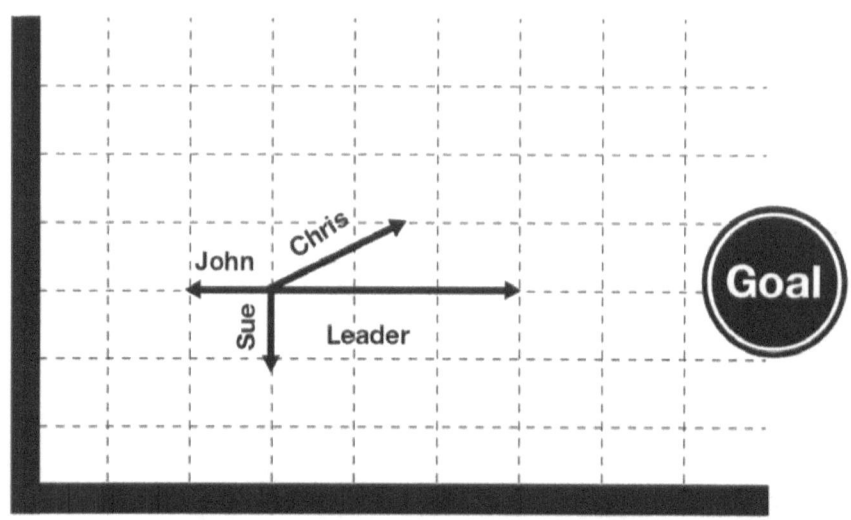

In Graphic 3, we see that our leader now has two additional team members, Sue and John. Sue is in a space where she doesn't really care what she does as long as she brings home a paycheck and is able to pay the bills, while John is mildly upset about being here as he feels it's just a lateral move and he's not inspired by the leader's direction. In fact, John is mildly opposed to where the team seems to be going. Now you may ask yourself what is the outcome or end-effect of the vector dynamics as depicted here. We will show this in the next graphics.

GRAPHIC 4:

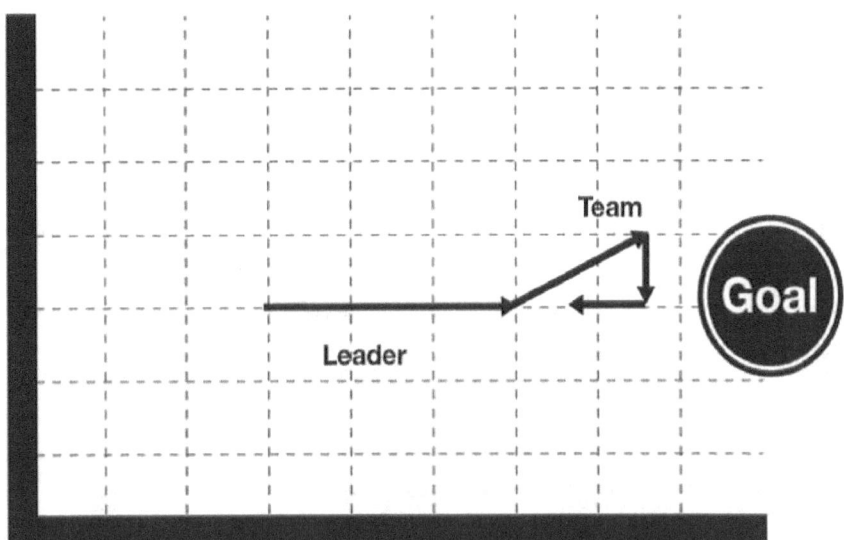

In Graphic 4, we have now added the vectors together by adding them end-to-end. By doing this, we get a clearer picture of how strongly this team will work toward the leader's goal. When we connect the starting point to the very end, we now have the actual level of push toward the leader's goal as depicted in Graphic 5.

GRAPHIC 5:

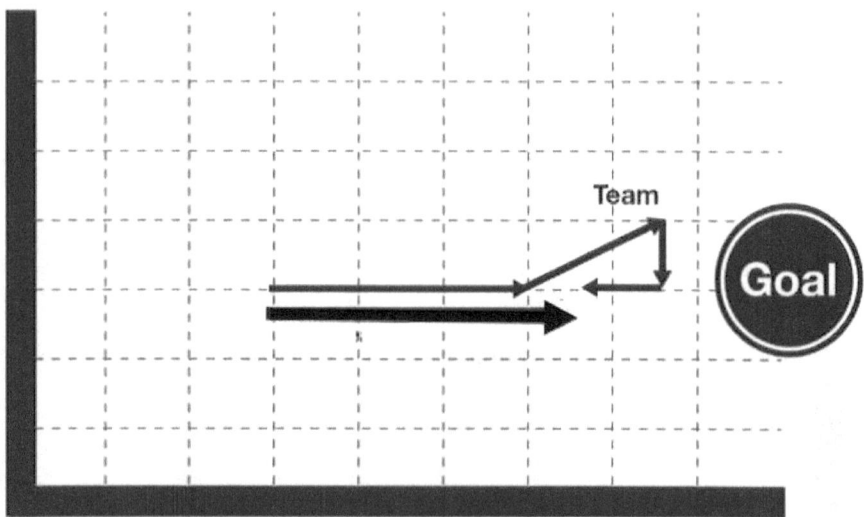

In Graphic 5, the summary and total push toward the leader's goal is represented by the thicker arrow. This is the sum total of the efforts of all the team members combined, including the leader. We have moved the arrow slightly lower to improve its visibility. In Graphic 5, you see that even though our leader has three members on her team, the combined push in this scenario is only a little bit greater than that of the leader working by herself.

The next question you will likely ask now is: What is the potential of this specific team if it were aligned in the same direction? Graphic 6 will answer this.

GRAPHIC 6:

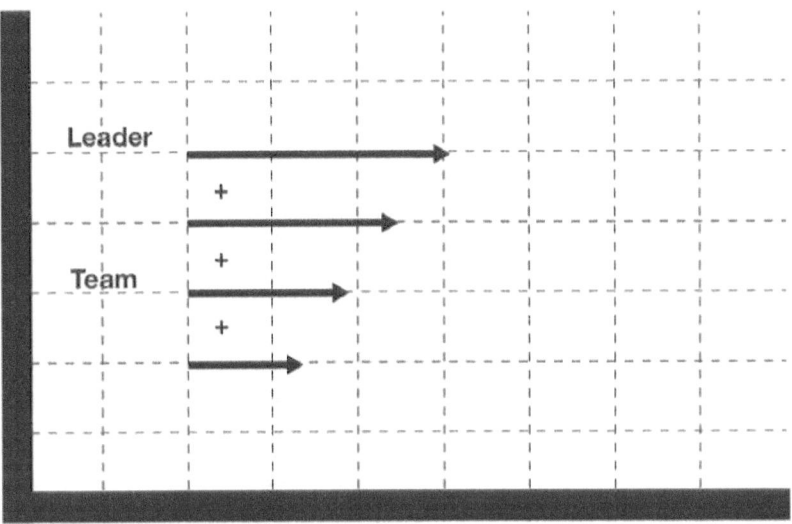

Here we have the individual vectors shown separately yet aligned with the leader. What happens when we add them up?

GRAPHIC 7:

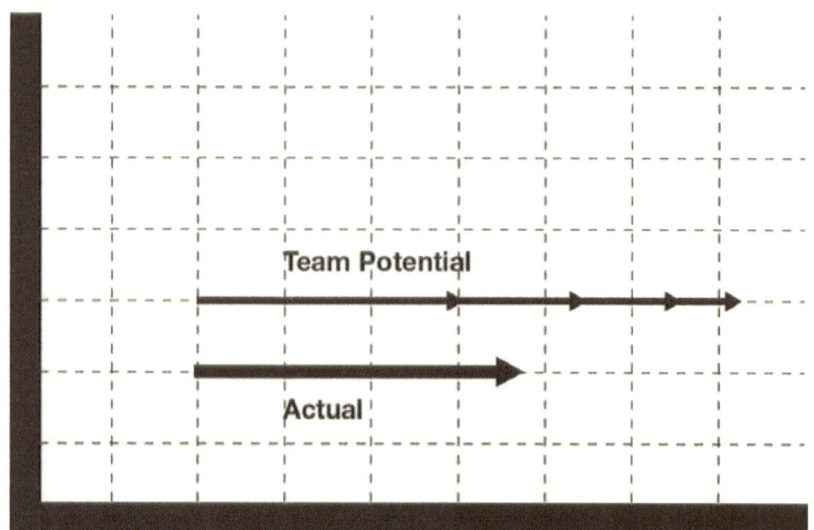

The upper combined arrows depict what the team potential would look like with full alignment. This does not yet include any increase in motivation generated by full team alignment. Truly aligned teams are a force with which to be reckoned. This particular team, through alignment, has now approximately doubled its push, energy, power or momentum in the direction of the leader's goal. Another way of looking at it is that it has practically doubled its momentum.

This can be quite an eye-opening read for those of us who are leading teams, groups or entire organizations. (Note: Actual results will vary depending on actual team composition and alignment!)

The principle of vector dynamics and alignment also applies to individuals, by the way. Even within ourselves, we'll find that we're not completely in alignment with certain goals or targets we have. (Not surprisingly, these are the areas where we experience a lot of struggle or stress in our efforts to succeed.) Once upon a long, long time ago I was up for a job at a higher level. Part of me wanted to get that higher-level job because it meant some more money; another part of me *didn't* want that job promotion because it also meant a lot more responsibility.

When there are internal conflicts like these, it's literally like having two rowers in the same boat going in completely opposite directions! And that's why even on the level of our individual selves, it's important that we find alignment.

Any opposing values, beliefs or attitudes will fight against us and ultimately slow us down or keep us from achieving our goals.

EXERCISE

Find one area in your life where you've experienced a lot of struggle or conflict. It could be your job or a project, it could be one of your relationships, or it could be anything else. Examine that area and identify what elements, desires or values are in conflict.

For example, maybe spending time on Facebook makes you happy, but it also distracts you from your work. Once you've identified the conflicting elements, see how you can create alignment. One option is to create priorities (e.g., work first, Facebook second); another option is to create boundaries (e.g., focus on Facebook only after work hours); yet another option is to eliminate a conflicting element entirely (e.g., delete your Facebook account). Or yet another option is to find a way to use Facebook in a way that supports your work!

Now, creating alignment isn't easy and it can involve making tough choices. But living without it is even harder. In the absence of alignment, energy is just wasted—and that leaves you with a lot less power to fulfill on what you really want.

>
> *We are what we repeatedly do. Excellence, therefore, is not an act but a habit.*
> **Aristotle**
>

We can see the importance of alignment in our endeavors and our previous formula for success will end up as:

ALIGNMENT x BEING x DOING = HAVING

With this formula, we achieve not only exponential leadership but also exponential results!

BUCKETS OF ENERGY

AN ADDITIONAL REASON why it's so critical to foster alignment within organizations is the simple fact that people are connected. We're sure you've noticed that in any given team within an organization, people start with various levels of energy and these levels don't remain static. Over time, the people who started with an elevated level of energy will have their energy level lowered and the people who started with a low level of energy will have their energy level raised. The impact of what energy levels exist and how things are done and what is accomplished are tremendous as we have shown in our client engagements that produced tremendous results and even won global awards.

Why?

As we said earlier, we're all connected. One way of visualizing this connection is to first imagine a series of buckets with each bucket containing a different level of "liquid" or energy. If the buckets remain separated, nothing happens. But once the buckets are connected, something happens...

As shown in the illustration above, the level of liquid within the buckets begins to equalize, leaving each bucket with an equal amount of liquid.

The energy levels of leaders will have an understandably disproportionate impact on their teams. A low energy leader will significantly lower the team's average level of energy while a high energy leader will significantly increase the team's average level of energy.

Given all this, it's vitally important to ensure that employees are aligned and empowered across the board. Otherwise, the misaligned and the disempowered will drag the group's energy down!

CRAFTING YOUR PURPOSE

IN HIS BEST-SELLING book *The Fifth Discipline: The Art and Practice of the Learning Organization*, Peter Senge talks about the three ideas that animate and govern the life of an organization: its vision, its purpose and its values. In this major section of this book, we'll be examining each of these three in turn. We will start with purpose.

If an organization's vision is its response to the question "What do we want to create?", its purpose is its response to the question "Why do we exist?"

In the broadest terms, purpose can be defined as the reason for which an organization exists. Articulating or defining an organization's purpose provides many short-term and long-term benefits, but we'll only stress the two most important benefits here.

First, having a purpose provides enormous energy, inspiration and motivation. Knowing that the existence of an organization fulfills something or contributes something to the world outside of or in addition to making money is tremendously inspiring. Organizations with purposes that go beyond simply making money grow *thrice* as fast as their competitors! All this has to do with the energy, inspiration and motivation that having a purpose provides.

Second, having a purpose simplifies things. A purpose defines what an organization does and doesn't do. It becomes the standard by which to evaluate which activities are essential and which aren't. One simply asks, "Does this activity help my organization fulfill its purpose?"

Without a clear purpose, there is no foundation upon which to base decisions, allocate time and use resources. Instead, organizational choices will be based on the circumstances, needs and pressures of the moment. Organizations that aren't clear about their purpose do too many things and scatter their employees' energies in too many different directions. It's this lack of focus that causes employees to feel confused, fatigued, overwhelmed, stressed and uninspired. A purpose funnels time, energy and attention by dictating what actions to take and what strategies to pursue.

Hence, the importance of having a purpose cannot be overemphasized. An organization's time, energy and resources are limited—if they are to count for something, the organization's members need to get clear as soon as possible about the purpose that their organization wants to accomplish. Just like the best visions, the best purposes are short, simple and easy to remember. For example, the purpose of Disney which is "Making People Happy!" consists of just three words!

> ### THE DIFFERENCE BETWEEN A PURPOSE AND A MISSION
>
> An Asian sea transport company decided that its mission was to provide the best sea passenger transport services available in the Philippines. When the company created its mission, it was the largest in its industry; and outperforming its direct competitors seemed like the most solid approach to securing its future.
>
> Unfortunately, a completely unexpected competitor appeared. This competitor's services were slightly more expensive, but it reduced what used to be a ten-hour trip from Manila to Cebu to just about an hour and a half. People noticed very quickly that for just a few hundred pesos more, they could save themselves at least eight hours of travel time—while traveling in air-conditioned comfort.
>
> What had happened? Simply speaking, a new low-cost airline had appeared. The sea transport company's revenues dropped rapidly and dramatically, and it barely managed to survive.

What happened to this company was what typically happens when organizations focus on a narrow-minded mission rather than on a purpose.

In simple terms, a mission contains a very specific articulation about HOW a company is to fulfill its vision. A purpose, on the other hand, simply states WHAT a company aims to provide to fulfill its vision. In the case of the sea transport company, for example, it had articulated its mission as transporting people BY SEA. If it had chosen to formulate its purpose instead as, say, providing customers with a means of getting from point A to point B in the most comfortable and convenient way, it would not have been limited to sea transport but to all kinds of transport. It might even have taken the initiative of launching its own budget airline! But limited thinking due to their mission didn't permit it nor did it care as well as it could have about the customer experience.

Therefore we ultimately recommend that organizations formulate a purpose rather than a mission. The narrower focus of a mission limits what's possible for an organization—both in terms of its ability to identify opportunities and to anticipate threats. And, as demonstrated by what happened to the sea transport company, the results of such a limitation can be devastating.

CRAFTING YOUR VISION

AN ORGANIZATION'S VISION is its response to the question "What do we want to create and achieve?" Visions provide some things for an organization, the most important of which are the following:

1. **Visions allow the organization to focus its attention and its resources.** A vision articulates the larger goal that underlies all an organization's efforts. Without a vision, an organization can easily disperse its energies and resources across a wide variety of activities that have no synergies at best or contradict each other at worst. This not only leads to ineffectiveness and inefficiency but also causes confusion, dissipates energy and even undermines morale.

2. **Visions allow the organization to achieve unity in diversity.** A vision provides the most

fundamental basis of commonality across the various levels and diverse groups of an organization. Without imposing conformity, it allows the members of an organization to become a coherent and connected unit that can use the different capabilities at its disposal in the fulfillment of a shared aspiration. By serving as the basis of a shared identity, visions foster a sense of ownership in the organization—turning what would otherwise be thought of as "their" company to "our" company.

3. **Visions provide energy and motivation.** As Mr. Senge points out, organizations derive their energy from two basic sources of motivation: the first is fear; the second is aspiration. While fear releases energy that can be remarkably effective in the short-term, only aspiration unleashes the kind of energy that endures. A good vision expresses how the organization ultimately seeks to make a difference or provide real value to the world. By painting a grand enough picture that transcends all the tiny, everyday details, visions provoke passion and generate inspiration.

THE DIFFERENCE BETWEEN COMPLIANCE AND COMMITMENT

Compliance and commitment are on the opposite ends of the spectrum of ways by which people can relate to a vision. Mr. Senge lists these ways as follows:

a. **Compliance.** This is the most common response. With compliance, people accept the vision and do what's asked of them—but *only* what's asked of them.

b. **Enrollment.** Enrollment involves a much higher level of ownership than compliance. With enrollment, people choose the vision and they do whatever they can do to fulfill it—but *only* within the limits set by their responsibilities within the organization.

c. **Commitment.** Commitment involves the highest level of ownership of a vision. With commitment, people *desire* the vision and they do whatever they can do to fulfill it—*even* creating innovative approaches and establishing new systems if necessary.

Obviously, an organization made up of people who are enrolled in or committed to its vision will perform at a profoundly higher level than an organization made up of people who are just complying with the vision. This is because enrollment and commitment involve initiative: enrolled and committed individuals will act on *their* own to bring a vision to life. The more an organization's members move from enrollment to commitment, however, the more the organization benefits from its people's initiative and from the creativity, excitement and passion that usually accompany such initiative.

Unfortunately, most organizations will settle for compliance. One reason for this is that many organizations are accustomed to having a culture of compliance. Another, perhaps more important, reason is that many organizations simply do *not* know how to direct and manage the energy that is unleashed by enrollment and commitment. For organizations that are willing to have their members enrolled in or committed to their visions, the following guidelines are helpful:

a. **The leaders must be enrolled in or committed to the vision themselves!** If the leaders of an organization aren't inspired by the vision, how can they expect the same vision to inspire their teams?

b. **The leaders must be honest about the risks and rewards of the vision.** The leaders of the organization must state the pros and cons of the vision as simply and candidly as they can. Inflating a vision's rewards or downplaying its risks only runs the risk of causing future disillusionment and even outright rejection.

c. **The leaders must allow the members of the organization to choose genuinely.** Compliance is all that is possible in the absence of genuine choice. If an organization, for whatever pressing reason, does not have the time needed for enrollment or commitment to develop, it can, at the very least, be honest about needing immediate compliance. This kind of authenticity and candor will make it easier for the organization's members to not just comply with the vision, but to even be enrolled in it to some degree, committed to it—and even possibly be inspired by it.

Having said all of the above, it must be noted that there is no one guaranteed formula for creating enrollment or commitment. The most an organization can ultimately do is to create the conditions favorable for enrollment and commitment to happen. When we work with organizations, we diligently diagnose the current situation, reality and relationships and base our recommendations on our findings.

THE PROFOUND IMPORTANCE OF A FUTURE ORIENTATION

In race car driving, a good deal of success depends on the driver's ability to keep track of what's right ahead of his car while also keeping the horizon in his perspective. Too shortsighted a focus means being unable to see obstacles until it's too late. Too farsighted a focus, on the other hand, means losing sight of nearby obstacles altogether.

Just like race car drivers, organizations must maintain a present, short-term and a future orientation. Developing a corporate culture that is truly future-oriented, however, is admittedly challenging.

First, the needs of the present need to be juggled along with the opportunities for the future. The present offers enough difficulties as it is with fires to be fought, results to be accomplished and shareholders to be placated, among many other things.

Second, anticipating the shape of the future itself is getting increasingly problematic as the rate of change in our societies accelerates. In the past, a future orientation meant anticipating how things would look over the next ten to twenty years. These days, profound changes can completely alter the state of entire industries in spans of time as short as two to three years, or even less.

Regardless of how challenging it is, however, an organization cannot survive—let alone thrive—without a profound orientation towards the future. Such an orientation will not only require the ability to look ahead but the willingness to forego tried and tested ways of doing things. Fortunately, or unfortunately, as the pace of change accelerates, completely unprecedented challenges will arise that will require radically new solutions. While venturing into the unknown is risky, it's ultimately riskier to insist on doing things in the same old ways when the circumstances have drastically changed. It is, to put it quite bluntly, an inability to evolve that will literally lead to extinction.

How Effective Visions Can Be Crated

Mr. Senge recommends following the principles below in crafting an organizational vision:

1. **Encourage the development of personal visions.** Ultimately, shared visions emerge from individual visions—the personal aspirations and dreams of an organization's members. If an organization's vision does not resonate with its members' personal visions, its members will simply *comply* with the group vision rather than commit to it.

   For this reason, the development of a shared vision has to include *all* levels within the organization. Being a leader within the organization does not mean possessing a monopoly on the vision. Rather, it means shouldering the responsibility of overseeing the visioning *process*. Gone are the days when "leaders" can issue visions from on high and expect obedience. These days, if leaders feel strongly about *their* personal visions, they need to possess the humility needed to share their visions and to ask for support.

   This, in turn, is the single biggest reason why shared visions cannot be developed overnight. Organization leaders can sometimes insist on fitting the visioning process into a fixed and narrow timetable. However, the members of an organization need be given enough time to understand the proposed vision and to see how it relates to their own personal visions.

Having said all of the foregoing, it must be noted that it is impossible to force people to accept a vision or to even develop personal visions of their own! The most that an organization can do is to create a climate that fosters the development of visions. Organizational leaders can model the desired behavior by communicating their own visions in a way that encourages others to create and share their own visions. This is what Mr. Senge refers to as the art of "visionary leadership."

2. **Allow multiple visions to coexist.** As counter-intuitive as it may sound, creating a shared vision actually involves allowing "multiple visions to coexist," as Mr. Senge puts it. The fact is, the members of an organization will connect to the group vision in their own unique way, resulting in multiple visions that are (hopefully) just minor variations of a single theme. Insisting on having people relate to the group vision in just a single, precise way will once again merely result in compliance and not commitment. Creating a shared vision, therefore, requires the willingness to respect a diversity of ideas, focusing on what ultimately "transcends and unifies all [the] individual visions." This is why when we work with organizations that are in the process of crafting their visions, we think of our task as simply listening to what the organization as a whole is trying to say—and then ensuring that what it's saying is subsequently powerfully articulated.

ONE POSSIBLE METHOD FOR CRAFTING A PERSONAL VISION

People often wonder about how to actually begin the process of crafting a personal vision. A starting point we recommend is inspired by a quote from Tesla founder Elon Muskwho said: "I don't want to save the world. I just want to think about the future and not be sad."

If you're struggling with creating your own personal vision, we invite you to look in the mirror, gaze deeply into your own eyes, and honestly ask yourself:

- ☐ What's a future I can envision that won't make me sad?
- ☐ How can I personally contribute to creating this future?

And if you'd like to go even further, even if it's just speculation, you can ask:

- ☐ What's a future that my team can envision that won't make them sad?
- ☐ What can my team contribute to creating this future?

Once you've completed your speculation and are ready to write down your vision, remember to keep your vision short and simple. If your vision is too wordy, you won't be able to remember it. And if you can't remember it, how can you enact it in the world?

3. **View visioning work as a process that never ends.** Grand vision setting exercises often create the impression that vision-setting only happens once—that once the vision is written, the work of visioning stops. However, writing the vision only starts the process. The rest of the process is about making the vision come alive and this is a task that never ends.

As Bill O'Brien once put it: "Being a visionary leader is not about giving speeches and inspiring the troops. How I spend my day is pretty much the same as how any executive spends his day. Being a visionary leader is about solving day-to-day problems with my vision in mind." In short, vision-setting might sound glamorous and exciting, but much of the work involved happens every day in the mundane and ordinary things.

For Mr. Senge, the visioning process can be thought of as a virtuous circle that works in the following way: "Visions spread because of a reinforcing process of increased clarity, enthusiasm, communication and commitment. As people talk, the vision grows clearer. As it gets clearer, enthusiasm for its benefits builds. And soon, the vision starts to spread in a reinforcing spiral of communication and excitement."

However, this virtuous circle can be hampered or limited by a number of things. Mr. Senge describes these restraining influences and their prescribed solutions as follows:

a. **As more people get involved in the visioning process, the diversity of their views dissipates focus and creates conflict.** What will be critical in sustaining the visioning process here is an ability to harmonize the inevitable diversity of views—an ability that requires being able to "inquire into diverse visions in such a way that deeper, common visions emerge."

b. **As clarity of the vision grows, clarity of the gap between the vision and current reality also grows—leading to uncertainty, discouragement and even cynicism.** What will be critical in sustaining the visioning process, in this case, is an ability to hold what Mr. Senge refers to as "creative tension." Mr. Senge describes creative tension as the "tension between vision and reality," and he asserts that the most effective people "are those who can 'hold' their vision while remaining committed to seeing current reality clearly." The ability to hold creative tension allows for sustained commitment to a lofty vision.

c. **As people work on addressing the demands of current reality, they get overwhelmed by these demands and lose focus on the vision.** What will be critical in sustaining the visioning process here is having enough organizational time and resources to work on fulfilling the vision. On the most practical level, it means separating the work of managing current reality and the work of making the vision real.

d. **As the visioning work proceeds, people lose their sense of connectedness to each other and the space needed for genuine connection to the shared vision disappears.** What will be critical in sustaining the visioning process, in this case, is ensuring that the people involved have the time and the skills needed for the connection to happen. If there's not enough time, people will be forced to rush through the process, resulting in mere compliance with the vision—if not outright resentment. At the same time, involvement in visioning work requires certain skills, such as the ability to communicate a vision, lead an inquiry and encourage reflection. Without these skills, the connection needed for the visioning process to continue will either fail to be established or will wither away altogether.

EVALUATING WHERE YOUR ORGANIZATION STANDS WITH REGARD TO ITS VISION

When we work with organizations to evaluate where they stand in relation to their visions, we often frame what we see in terms of alignment and misalignment. The more people are aligned with the vision, the more empowered they will be and the better the organization's performance will be. The fewer people are aligned with the vision, the more disempowered they will be and the poorer the organization's performance will be.

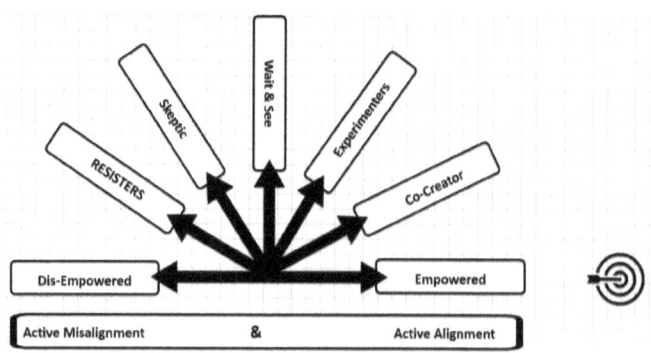

Over the years, we've learned to categorize an organization's employees in terms of their level of alignment (or misalignment) with the vision:

1. **The Empowered.** These are the members of the organization who are fully aligned with its vision, are fully

empowered, and can be trusted to do the right things on their own to produce the desired outcomes.

2. **The Co-Creators.** These are the people who are more or less aligned with the vision but disagree with it in minor respects. As a result of these slight divergences, they can initiate minor "course corrections" that can impact the desired outcomes.

3. **The Experimenters.** These are the people who have greater disagreements with the vision than the Co-Creators. Because of these greater divergences in thought, they can create new approaches independently and without the consensus of the rest of the group. While such experimentation isn't bad in itself, the failure to solicit input from the rest of the group can result in narrow perspectives that can lead to failure.

4. **Wait and See.** These are the people who neither agree nor disagree with the vision and are simply "sitting on the fence." This casual or indifferent attitude translates to wasting of time and a dissipation of energy. For such employees, it's best to get them "off the fence" and aligned with the vision as soon as possible.

5. **The Skeptics.** These are the people who don't believe in the vision altogether and as a result of their skepticism can be very challenging to work with.

6. **The Resisters.** These are the people who not only disagree with the vision—they also actively express their disagreement and slow things down in various ways through their outright resistance.

7. **The Disempowered.** These are the people who hardly have enough energy to get out of their own way and therefore pose a lesser challenge than the Resisters. However, whatever little energy they do have left will usually go into resistance.

Understanding the groups to which employees belong, and the relative sizes of these groups will allow you to determine what steps to take to achieve active alignment within an organization. The good news though is that most of the Wait and See people, the Skeptics, the Resisters and the Disempowered can be "turned around" if they are spotted early enough. Ideally, an organization should work towards cultivating the kinds of conditions where employees do not develop such states of misalignment in the first place!

What Causes Visions To Fail

The growing recognition of the power of vision has compelled many organizations to work extensively on developing statements of their visions. However, the visions resulting from such work often fail to produce their intended benefits. The key reasons for such failures include the following:

1. **Most organizational visions are merely the visions of certain individuals versus truly shared visions.** One of the most common vision-related problems faced by organizations is the fact that their visions are typically just the vision of one person or one group that is then imposed or cascaded down to the rest of the organization. This leads to what we would refer to as a culture of drudging compliance rather than a culture of daring commitment. While there is nothing wrong with compliance, compliance doesn't unleash the kind of creativity, energy, excitement, experimentation, initiative, innovation, inspiration, ownership and risk-taking that authentic commitment does. Hence, the challenge for most organizations is developing a truly shared vision—one that reflects the personal visions of the individuals that constitute it.

2. **Most organizational visions reflect extrinsic goals versus intrinsic goals.** According to Mr. Senge, many organizations articulate their visions in terms of goals that are functions of the external environment, i.e., attaining market leadership, defending market leadership, etc. While there is nothing wrong with such extrinsic goals, Mr. Senge points out that they can easily degenerate into defensive postures intended to maintain the status quo rather than inspiring actions focused on creating something truly new. On the other hand, intrinsic goals that are based on the organization's

internal standards—standards relating to excellence, integrity or customer satisfaction, for instance—are more powerful because they provoke a never-ending quest for fulfillment that considers not just tried-and-tested methods but also novel approaches.

3. **Most organizational visions are short-term and reactive versus long-term and proactive.** In his book, Mr. Senge cites the following quote by Gary Hamel of the London Business School and C.K. Prahalad of the University of Michigan: "Although strategic planning is billed as a way of becoming more future-oriented, most managers, when pressed, will admit that their strategic plans reveal more about today's problems than tomorrow's opportunities." Examples of such short-term and reactive visions are visions created to address a current problem. The problem with such visions is that when the problem is solved, the vision loses its power. Another problem with short-term and reactive visions is that they only inspire short-term and reactive actions. Only a long-term vision can create and foster long-term commitment. And more often than not, long-term visions articulate goals far worthier of commitment—and far more capable of inspiring commitment—than short-term ones.

A Final Word on Visions

In conclusion, as the concrete picture of what an organization is intending to create, visions provide focus, identity and inspiration. However, the task of creating a powerful, proactive and enduring vision that is truly shared is enormously challenging, and for this reason, many visions fail. While no guaranteed formula exists for creating a shared vision, guidelines are available for making the process easier. Hopefully, by following the guidelines that have been presented, your organization can succeed in its quest to craft an enormously empowering and truly shared vision.

ARTICULATING YOUR VALUES

IF AN ORGANIZATION'S vision is its response to the question "What do we want to create?", and its purpose is its response to the question "Why do we exist?", its values are its response to the question "How do want to operate?"

In his best-selling book *Awaken the Giant Within*, Anthony Robbins talks about values as the ultimate determinants of "our every decision and, therefore, our destiny." To give a simple and practical example, let's say that you want to go to Rome from Paris on your next holiday. Now, there are a number of ways you could get to Rome from Paris, i.e., fly a plane, take a train, go on a bus, drive a car, hitch a ride, and so on and so forth. Now, if adventure, economy and fun rank high on your travel values, you might easily choose to hitch a ride. If, on the other hand, convenience, safety and speed rank high on your travel values, you might automatically choose to fly a plane.

In short, values are the guiding principles that determine how an organization goes about attaining its vision and pursuing its purpose. Now, what complicates the matter of values—and what makes them a frequent subject in the area of training and development—is two things:

The first is that organizations are very rarely clear about their own values and the hierarchy of their values. Said another way, organizations are often unclear about the principles that they find truly important. If they do happen to be clear about the principles that matter, they're often not clear about how these principles stand in relation to each other. The consequences of such a lack of clarity include difficulties in making decisions and inconsistencies in taking action.

For example, one of the most famous case studies in business ethics courses is about how John Pepper, the former Chairman of the Board of Procter & Gamble or P&G for short, discovered that one of P&G's contractors had been searching through the rubbish bins of rival firm Unilever and had found sensitive information about the latter's competitive strategy. Mr. Pepper immediately fired the executives who had been responsible for the espionage—then went directly to Unilever to acknowledge the deed and to provide reassurance that the information would not be used. Unilever, understandably enough, reacted to the disclosure by threatening to take legal action against P&G if a settlement involving the payment of $10 to 20 million in damages, among other things, was not quickly reached.

Why this case is so instructive in a discussion regarding values is because Mr. Pepper's decision and consequent action were clearly dictated by values. To this day, industry observers remain divided about P&G's disclosure of its espionage to Unilever. Some analysts believe that P&G did the right thing in confessing the misdemeanor; others believe that the disclosure was a gross mistake and that Unilever had brought the incident upon itself by being careless with its information in the first place.

Now, if P&G's top management had not been clear about the company's values and their priorities, it would have been very difficult to decide how to deal with the situation—especially since the two options involved had significant tradeoffs. But since P&G's top management was clear that it valued honesty, integrity and transparency, it acted in accordance with these values even if it came at great cost and risk. This underlines one of the most powerful benefits of being clear about the values of one's organization—which is that values make the decision-making process vastly simpler by dictating what one should do in any particular situation.
Even organizations that have clarified and prioritized their values can still experience difficulty in making decisions. This brings us to the second thing that complicates the matter of values, which is that even when values and their relations to each other are clear, it can be very challenging to honor them.

The challenge can come from many sources. One common source is a lack of external support for the company's values, which is what happened to a certain extent in the case above with P&G. Another common source is an internal conflict between two closely ranked values. Again, in the P&G case mentioned, there was very likely a good degree of internal conflict in the lower levels of management between the desire to do the right thing and the desire to protect the company's reputation.

Although the pressures of the marketplace can make it tempting to perpetually postpone the work of clarifying organizational values, doing it is probably one of the most critical things that can be done to ensure the organization's long-term success.

First, clarifying values provides insight into why an organization's employees consistently act the way they do, since corporate values implicitly (if not explicitly) guide employee behavior. Second, such work provides insight into why employees experience conflict in making particular decisions since mutually-exclusive values held in equal regard can paralyze decision-making. Third, clear values provide a framework that can be used to maximize organizational success. Meaning, if an organization is clear about its values but is not acting consistently with them, that inconsistency is already a clear cause of failure.

Such failures to act by a stated set of values often occur when organizations buckle to profit-making pressures and pursue their bottom lines at the expense of their values and their integrity. These failures ALWAYS cost the company severely in the long run, either through exorbitant litigation fees or lost consumer trust.

For example, in September 2015, the United States' Environmental Protection Agency (EPA) discovered that Volkswagen had outfitted its diesel engines with software that could detect when the car was being tested—and change the car's performance accordingly to improve results. In effect, Volkswagen's diesel cars were designed to meet test standards but failed to meet these same standards in real-world conditions. Investigations understandably spread to other countries and, soon enough, environmental, governmental and regulatory groups around the world began questioning the legitimacy of Volkswagen's emissions testing. By the end of the scandal, Volkswagen ended up having to recall 500,000 cars in the United States and *8.5 million* cars in Europe—including 2.4 million in Germany and 1.2 million in the United Kingdom. The carmaker's shares fell by about a third and it posted its first quarterly loss in fifteen years of €2.5 billion in October 2015. Most importantly, as the company's then Chief Executive Officer Martin Winterkorn said: Volkswagen had "broken the trust of [its] customers and the public."

Volkswagen is far from being the first or the only company to have betrayed its own values for the sake of profitability. But the point is, in a day and age when information and communications technologies have become so pervasive, it's become extremely challenging if not downright impossible for organizations to conceal their misdemeanors from the public. In a very authentic way, information and communication technology has changed the landscape to such an extent that companies don't need to adhere to their values just to thrive—they need to adhere to their values to survive.

Now, if an organization is clear about its values but is experiencing a conflict between two or more of them, it can either pursue the most important values first or do the challenging work of finding a way to fulfill all its values. This work can take a lot of courage, experimentation, ingenuity and patience, but if an organization succeeds in doing so, it will have found a way of operating that allows it to maintain its integrity—paving the way for its employees to find an abiding fulfillment, pride and satisfaction in their work.

THE DIFFERENCE BETWEEN VALUES AND RULES

Some organizations are run according to rules and some are run according to values. The difference between these two is similar to the difference between a mission and a purpose.

Simply put, rules are explicitly-stated principles that govern behavior within a particular domain while values are foundational principles that provide the basis for behavior within all relevant domains. While rules provide guidance on how one should conduct oneself in very specific situations, values provide guidance on how one should conduct oneself in *all* kinds of situations. This means that a company run according to rules will need to develop, disseminate and enforce hundreds—if not *thousands*—of rules to ensure that its employees behave *correctly*, while a company run according to values will need to identify, share and embody just a handful of values to ensure that its employees behave *appropriately*.

Said another way, rules belong to the realm of DOING and are appropriate for the old, Industrial Revolution-based, assembly line method of doing things, while values

> belong to the realm of BEING and are more appropriate for the new, Information Revolution-based, non-linear way of doing things. Rules rely on conformity and obedience whereas values rely on fidelity and commitment. The former breeds servility and dependence while the latter unleashes creativity and engagement.
>
> It's easy to tell which we need more of in today's world! As Victoria puts it, "Great leadership is distinguished by values, not rules."

How to Identify and Prioritize an Organization's Values

Given the critical importance of values, let's proceed to the fundamental exercise of identifying and prioritizing an organization's values.

As described previously, values are the principles that organizations deem as most important. To a substantial extent, an organization's values are determined by its history and its values can change as circumstances change. For example, a company established by an enterprising and visionary founder is very likely to value independence and initiative in its employees. If independence and initiative lead to too many impulsive and ultimately unsuccessful ventures, however, the organization's values may shift more towards collaboration and caution.

Why it's important to know the above is because: (1) knowing the origins of an organization gives us a good place to start from when identifying its values; and (2) recognizing that values change as circumstances change tells us that an organization should periodically review its list of values and the hierarchy of its values.

In relation to the second point above, we'd like to propose a distinction between past-based values and future-based values. Past-based values refer to the principles that have allowed an organization to be successful up to the present. Past-based values, however, may no longer be appropriate in fulfilling the organization's vision for the future. As we mentioned earlier, fulfilling its vision may require the organization to depart radically from what it used to be and how it used to do things.

Having said the preceding, let's now finally proceed with learning how to identify and prioritize an organization's values.

1. The first and most important step is for the leadership team to develop an inspiring purpose and vision.

2. The second step is for the leadership team to come up with a preliminary list of what they believe the organization's values are. This is the easy step and should not take more than ten or fifteen minutes. Some of the corporate values we encounter quite frequently include collaboration, commitment, excellence, innovation, integrity, leadership, people, quality, responsibility and service. Values should be just one word and should express ways of being rather than ways of doing.

3. The third step is for the leadership team to examine its preliminary list of values and to determine if these values are appropriate given its vision, its purpose and its objectives. At this stage, the team may need to remove certain values and add new ones.

4. The fourth step is for the leadership team to streamline and define its values. According to science, the human mind cannot easily recall more than six things at a time. Hence, the team should select *no more than six* core values. If it has more than six values, it should see whether some values can be combined into a single value. Once the team has identified its final list of values, it should then clearly define what each value means to avoid any risk of future misinterpretation.

5. The fifth step is for the leadership team to rank its final list of values. This step is a lot more challenging than the second step! Regardless of how difficult it is, however, the leadership team *must resist* the temptation to assign the same rank to two or more values. Values must have a clear hierarchy, and the more firmly this hierarchy is established, the better the organization's chances of avoiding dilemmas later on. Remember: any difficulty organizations experience in making decisions ultimately comes from a lack of clarity with regard to its values. At the same time, given that these values will serve as the organization's guide in future decision-making, the leadership team should ensure that they undertake the exercise carefully and with due consideration.

6. The sixth and final step, which requires a bit more time to accomplish, is for the leadership team to ensure that its organization's values are embodied and expressed by its employees. That is, checks should be done every so often at various levels of the organization to evaluate if employees are making decisions that are consistent with the company's values. If inconsistencies are discovered—and if there are *glaring* inconsistencies, in particular—the leadership team should aim to either shift how employees behave, or, alter the list or the hierarchy of the organization's values altogether.

How to Prepare for a Successful Purpose-Vision-Values-Setting Session

We mentioned earlier that the work of creating or recreating an organization's purpose, vision and values cannot and should not be rushed. Having said that, much time and energy can be saved by creating the conditions in which the purpose, vision and values can be set in a successful session. To create these conditions, we recommend the following:

1. **Create opportunities for leadership team members to get to know each other well; to develop trust in each other's abilities and expertise; to leave behind any past antagonisms; and to communicate and clear up any other critical issues that might impair frank and honest communication.** If the members of the leadership team barely know each other, or don't trust each other, or have lingering hostilities and resentments, it's highly unlikely that they'll succeed in the work of crafting a final

purpose, vision and set of values. Or if they do succeed, it's highly unlikely that these statements can actually be successfully communicated, disseminated and embodied by the rest of the organization.

2. **Encourage leadership team members to be willing to dream big and to play big.** Share stories from the organization's own past or from other organizations about what's possible when people let go of their self-imposed limits or their own individual concerns. If the people setting the organization's purpose, vision and values are playing small or are simply concerned about their own agendas, it's highly unlikely that the resulting statements will be able to inspire greatness or ownership among the organization's employees.

3. **Encourage leadership team members to be willing to let go of what's worked in the past.** As we've mentioned earlier, it's crucial for the leadership team to let go of past ways of seeing and doing things—regardless of how well they've worked—and to be willing to adopt new ways of seeing and doing things based on what's needed by the organization's present circumstances.

TIMING OF GROWTH INTERVENTIONS AND WHY MOST CHANGE EFFORTS FAIL

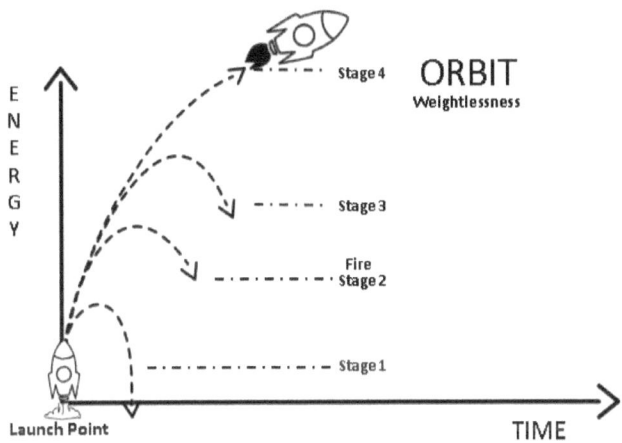

WHEN INTERVENTIONS AND growth programs fail, this failure can be driven by a number of reasons besides the program leader's lack of skill.

One critical reason is that interventions are often approached with a "one-shot-will-do-it" mindset much like a vaccine. However, this does not apply to learning and development. As the saying goes, it's the constant dripping of water that weathers a stone. A series of well-timed sessions is far more effective than a single one-time-big-time intervention. The ideal time tends to be every four to six weeks for the initial interventions and then every six to twelve months afterwards depending on the team's needs. After all, even some vaccines need booster shots!

THE 6 + 1 DRIVERS OF ENGAGEMENT

IN AN EARLIER section of this book, we described the phenomenon of Command-and-Control Leadership as the type of leadership that predominates in organizational cultures that view employees as mere cogs in a well-oiled machine. This view is a legacy of the old, Industrial Revolution-based, assembly line method of doing things, and can still be seen in our use of the phrase "human resources" to refer to an organization's employees! That is, people are literally resources to be used up in the process of fulfilling the organization's objectives! And because these human resources are limited, they need to be managed.

But the fact is: people aren't resources—and therefore can't be "managed." *Things* are resources and that's why things can be managed. Organizations ultimately fail to unleash the true potential of their employees when they simply relate to their employees as living and breathing *things* that need to be managed. If organizations want to unleash their employees' full creativity, engagement and ownership, they need to stop managing their employees as organic parts or as human "doings"— they need to start leading them as thinking and feeling human *beings*.

In this section of the book, we'll look at exactly how to do that.

What Employees Really Want and Need

Attracting and retaining the best employees in today's marketplace is becoming exceedingly challenging. Employees today routinely switch jobs, or, demand higher and higher salaries to stay in their current jobs.

In our work with a number of the world's Fortune 500 companies, we've discovered what it takes to hold on to the "keepers" without necessarily giving away the store. Unsurprisingly, these strategies for attracting and retaining great employees are based on meeting the four needs that underpin human happiness and the two additional needs that underpin human fulfillment. These needs are:

1. **The Need for Connection and Concern.** Working in an environment where one feels uncared for is one of the most demoralizing experiences one can possibly have. Employees who don't feel cared for will understandably not care for their organization, its purpose, its vision and its values. Showing genuine care and concern for one's employees can be done through many ways, including but not limited to paying close attention to one's subordinates, constantly listening to them and giving constructive feedback, supporting both their professional and their personal goals, and managing their workload so they're not overworked. According to recent research conducted at Stanford University, productivity per hour declines sharply when the work week exceeds 50 hours—and productivity drops off so much after 55 hours that nothing is gained out of working more!

> ### GENUINE CONCERN MEANS INTUITING THE UNSAID
>
> Employees often don't fully express themselves to their superiors. This isn't just because they don't *want* to do it—it can also be because they don't know *how* to do it. They may lack the ability to express themselves or they may feel it's not okay to express themselves. A truly concerned leader, however, is one who's able to "hear" what employees leave unsaid and act in ways that address the unspoken concern.

2. **The Need for Certainty.** With the rate of change accelerating in societies around the world, employees are feeling increasingly anxious and insecure. They're plagued by concerns about whether they'll continue to be a fit for their roles, whether they'll be given a new assignment or a new team that they can't handle, whether they'll even have a job if the market changes or if their company gets acquired, and so on and so forth. People simply do not function very well in the face of rampant uncertainty. If people are given a sufficient amount of assurance, certainty and predictability, this gives them the space to feel safe and secure and to subsequently thrive.

3. **The Need for Significance.** People need to feel that they're special and that they're uniquely

valued. It doesn't actually cost anything to solicit someone's opinion, acknowledge their successes, pay them a compliment or praise them for something well done. But strangely enough, organizations don't acknowledge or celebrate their employees enough in these "small" yet incredibly meaningful ways. Recognition often simply takes the form of pay increases—which simply reinforces the implicit mindset that people's loyalty and productivity must be "bought" or purchased.

4. **The Need for Variety.** Quite frankly, no one wants to do the same thing all the time. Few things are as draining as having to endlessly and monotonously repeat a task or a set of tasks. Employee boredom is one of the greatest contributors to loss of interest and satisfaction in work, with a corresponding impact on employee performance, productivity and loyalty. Hence, organizations need to ensure that they provide their employees with work that possesses some degree of internal variety, or at least provide them with opportunities to try something different on occasion.

5. **The Need for Growth.** Gallup Chief Executive Officer Jim Clifton once said on a LinkedIn post that the most important thing that employees need from their organizations is the opportunity to do what they do best every day. When people are given roles or tasks that play to their strengths and that allow them to excel, they are profoundly motivated to grow. This growth, in turn, leads to greater performance, productivity and loyalty. For this reason, the world's greatest companies are always on the lookout for ways to help their employees grow, expand and develop.

6. **The Need for Contribution.** Employees want to feel that what they do makes a difference to their organization—and even to the world!—in a meaningful and positive way. Simply put, doing good makes people feel good! The exact opposite of this is what happens when an organization engages in underhanded corporate practices that actually make its employees feel *bad*—therefore undermining their personal sense of integrity, their morale and their loyalty.

Now, when an organization is able to meet even just three of the above needs, its employees can easily find their jobs addicting—which is why so many non-profit workers stay in their roles despite their often miserable salaries. However, when employees don't have the above needs fulfilled, they turn to the most common substitute which is (yes, you guessed it), money. And if the organization isn't in a position to give employees more money, then these employees go about looking for another employer—with consequences on how much an organization has to spend on recruitment and retraining.

In summary, even if ensuring that the above needs are met will require a lot from an organization in terms of attention, energy, time and money, it will literally cost the organization MORE to leave these needs unmet. Costs will escalate as companies need to hire more and to train more to continuously replace dissatisfied or underperforming employees. Hence, being able to attract and retain good employees is critical not just for an organization to thrive—but to even simply survive.

THE 6 + 1 DRIVERS

We talked about vector dynamics in a previous chapter, but it's also important to take them into account in the context of employee engagement. Most employee engagement surveys only look at employee happiness, but employee alignment is absolutely vital as well. Focusing on engagement without alignment is like measuring the speed of the race car without caring about its direction!

FINAL WORDS

THIS MAY BE the end of our book, however, it's also just the beginning of a new journey for you. With these tools in hand, you will not only be more informed but also more empowered. You now know how to take on growth from a developmental approach that can be used not just in the good times when funding is available, but especially in the bad times when we need to find and deploy other means to achieve our results.

There is a huge goldmine hidden within the undiscovered potential of people just waiting to be explored, empowered and unleashed. Why wait? Start the process now and don't worry about getting everything right immediately. Even small shifts can create huge results. One of our clients had to build an additional factory to satisfy the demand that was created during the time we worked with their people. They ended up growing very fast and needed to adjust their supply to keep up with the much higher demand for their offerings.

We wish you all the best in your endeavors, and should you require assistance, we are here for you always.

Bjorn and Victoria Martinoff

OTHER HELPFUL TOPICS

The Value of Coaching in Developing Exponential Breakthrough Leadership

Former Google Chief Executive Officer Eric Schmidt once said: "Everyone needs a coach."

People who disagree with this statement typically come from the point of view that only leaders who aren't performing well need a coach—and it's the coach's job to "fix" them. People who agree with this statement, on the other hand, usually come from the point of view that leaders who are performing at the top of their game not only need a coach, but *deserve* a coach.

The latter viewpoint is much more readily seen in the world of athletics. In sports, it's the amateurs who don't get coaches while the professionals have *several*—one coach for a specific area such as health, fitness, strategy, and so on and so forth. Naturally, the amateurs who don't invest in a coach tend to progress more slowly and are much less likely to ever become pros. This is why the more forward-thinking organizations invest in coaches for their top-notch leaders: they recognize that coaching isn't about fixing flaws—it's about improving performance. And while it can be a substantial investment, it's one that eventually pays off.

In this section, we'll provide some guidelines on how to maximize the return of your coaching investment:

1. **Get yourself the best coach your money can buy.** It's easy to save money by getting a less experienced or lesser-known coach. But an investment in a more experienced or highly-rated coach will generate a greater return on your investment simply because such a coach will have already worked with the heads of several successful organizations and will have therefore addressed some very challenging issues. The greater the number of successful leaders a coach has worked with, the more exposed they've been to the kinds of issues such leaders face. The other thing we'll emphasize here is that the kind of coach that you should invest in should also be determined by your level of responsibility within the organization.

COACHING: IT'S NOT ONE SIZE FITS ALL

In our years of working as executive coaches, we've learned to tell our clients this simple truth: one's coaching needs change as one moves up the corporate ladder. That is, the kind of coaching needed by mid-level managers are different from the kind of coaching needed by top-level executives.

For example, as people go higher up the organization, they will need coaches who:

- focus less on motivating the client and focus more on helping the client motivate *others*;
- possess a working knowledge of all the areas top-level executives need to oversee and influence (including but not limited to human resources, marketing, operations, sales, etc.);
- possess a working knowledge of organizational frameworks, structures and systems;
- possess a working knowledge of all the available leadership interventions (whether in the form of books, courses, seminars or trainings);
- possess a working knowledge of all the relevant dimensions of a person's life (including but not limited to career, health, finances, relationships, spirituality, etc.);

- are in touch with the most cutting-edge approaches and solutions;
- are able to provide options and perspectives rather than advice; and
- possess more confidence, experience, expertise and power.

On a practical level, it's also helpful to hire a different coach for different levels of leadership (or even within the same level) simply to maintain confidentiality or to avoid conflicts of interest.

Now, when you're hiring a coach for yourself or for your organization, it's best to treat their certification credentials as a first level "filter." That is, use their level of certification as a preliminary assessment. After that, focus on the results that they've produced as a way of making the final judgment. To be candid, some of the highest-paid coaches in the world today—such as Anthony Robbins and Marshall Goldsmith—aren't certified because they've been coaching since *before* certification was even available. It's said that Mr. Robbins charges his clients $1 to 3 million per year, and while that might sound exorbitant, it pays to bear in mind that his clients routinely make decisions that involve tens and even *hundreds* of millions of dollars at a time. In short, the higher the stakes are, the more powerful you want your coach to be!

2. **Play a big game.** Whatever goals you've been tasked to achieve by your organization, aim for attaining even *higher* ones in your work with your coach. You can keep these higher goals between you and your coach. The point is, a big game generates more inspiration and more ideas than a small game.

> ### PUSH VERSUS PULL
>
> My good friend Robert Kiyosaki once said: "A coach isn't your friend. A coach is there to push you beyond what you thought was possible or what you wouldn't do on your own."
>
> While I agree with Robert on the basics, I part ways with him in his use of the word "push." While it seems like a small thing, small things are of BIG importance when it comes to coaching. My problem with the word "push" is that it's synonymous with Force. If people have to be "pushed," it means they need to be motivated from the *outside* by the coach. What this means, in turn, is that they become dependent on the coach and ultimately Power-less on their own.
>
> Real coaching, on the other hand, is about inspiring people from within so that they're *pulled* by their own personal vision rather than *pushed* by their own personal coaches. The best coaches do this in a way that allows their clients to be independent of them and em-Powered on their own.

3. **Include what matters most to you.** Don't limit the conversation to just your professional goals or to what's expected of you. Talk to your coach about what's important to you *personally* and don't be shy about sharing how you feel. If everything's just about work, you'll end up having less creativity, less energy, less fun, less inspiration and less stamina. While it may feel strange to be completely candid and honest with your coach, the more your coach knows about you, the better they can support you. Moreover, you can rest assured that the best coaches always treat their conversations with their clients with the utmost confidentiality.

4. **Be open to new ways of seeing, doing and achieving.** One of the most valuable things a coach provides is a different perspective. No matter how accomplished you are in your field—or *precisely* because you're so accomplished in your field—you stop seeing what's new. And when you stop seeing what's new, you end up doing the same things in the same way and thereby achieve the same results at the same speed. When you work with a coach though, you get to see things newly—which means doing things differently and achieving breakthrough results in unprecedentedly shorter spans of time. So rather than seeing your coach's suggestions as insults to your mastery, think of them as recommendations coming from a valuably different viewpoint.

PRIDE AND WHAT IT WILL COST YOU

In our experience, one of the things that can really get in the way of an organization's growth is pride amongst its highest level executives. Pride not only prevents such people from seeking coaching—it can get in the way of their hearing what the coach has to say if they *do* end up getting a coach.

Now, pride isn't just an inflated sense of ego coming from an overrated belief in one's ability. Pride can also be the result of fear being disguised. That is, pride is the visible face of a number of invisible fears. Fears such as:

- the fear of being, or appearing, insufficient;
- the fear of not being good enough or capable enough;
- the fear of having our true self exposed (or the fear of being exposed as a fraud);
- the fear of looking bad;
- the fear of not looking good;
- the fear of what others might say;
- the fear of harming our own self-image; and
- the fear of being vulnerable.

In such cases, pride appears to protect us from the enemy, which is fear. But invariably, pride only prevents the person from learning and growing—and is therefore not the protector but the *real* enemy.

5. **Apply what you learn.** You can spend hours with your coach discussing the best ways to level up your game, but if you don't apply what you learn, nothing's going to happen. After all, the true value of coaching shows up in your work and in your life *between* coaching sessions, not *during* coaching sessions!

> ### THE VITAL IMPORTANCE OF TRAINING AND DEVELOPMENT
>
> In times of financial crisis, it's all too easy for companies to slash costs by cutting down on employee-related initiatives such as team building events and training and development programs.
>
> Unfortunately, such "savings" schemes end up costing the company far more in the long run as deteriorations in the quality of its work force begin making themselves felt in the organization's performance. The fact is, continuously improving its human capital is the only way that a company can sustainably grow. So while scrimping on people seems savvy in the short run, it's surefire self-sabotage in the long run!

How to Find and Keep the Employees One Wants and Needs

In the past, companies hired employees based on whether they possessed the right skills for the job or not. These days, however, hiring on the basis of skill sets alone is vastly insufficient—organizations also need to hire based on whether prospective employees possess the right attitude *and* personality or not.

Why? In simple terms, hiring someone who possesses the right attitude and the right personality for his or her job vastly increases his or her chances of success at that job. An organized and meticulous person is better suited for detail-oriented work while an extroverted and ebullient person is better suited for sales work.

Hence, organizations that take the time and effort to determine what kinds of attitudes and personalities are needed for various roles—by profiling employees who are very successful at what they do, for instance—can greatly increase the performance and productivity of their work forces. Of course, it's not always guaranteed that the supply of available talent in the marketplace can meet the organization's skill-attitude-personality needs, but not knowing what these needs are in the first place means not even being in a position to look for the right people, let alone find them.

Now, finding the right people is just one part of the equation; letting go of the wrong people is another. The fact is, keeping the wrong employees not only costs an organization money (in the form of paying undeserved salaries), but also undermines productivity and morale because such employees have a detrimental effect on the people *around* them. Hence, although letting go of an employee (or several employees) can feel like an unpleasant task, it may be the only way to guarantee the organization's continued success.

When considering whether to let an employee go or not, you can ask yourself (or your team) the following questions:

1. What are the benefits of keeping this employee?

2. What are the direct and indirect costs of keeping this employee? How will retaining them affect other employees? How will retaining them affect morale? What other issues may arise if we keep this employee?

3. What are the direct and indirect consequences of letting this employee go? If they go and work for our competition, how will that affect our company? What other issues may arise if we let this employee go?

4. Have we explored and deployed all options to help this employee stay? If not, whom can we ask to assist?

FACTORING IN MARKET PERFORMANCE WHEN EVALUATING EMPLOYEE PERFORMANCE

As with everything else in life, keeping the bigger picture in mind is critical when evaluating an employee's performance. That is, it's not enough to simply compare the results they produced in the current year with the results they produced in the previous year because results aren't produced in a vacuum.

Let us illustrate what we mean using an example.

We once worked with a company whose results went up from minus five percent to 34 percent in one year. That was a whopping difference of 39 percentage points—and of course the company celebrated wildly.

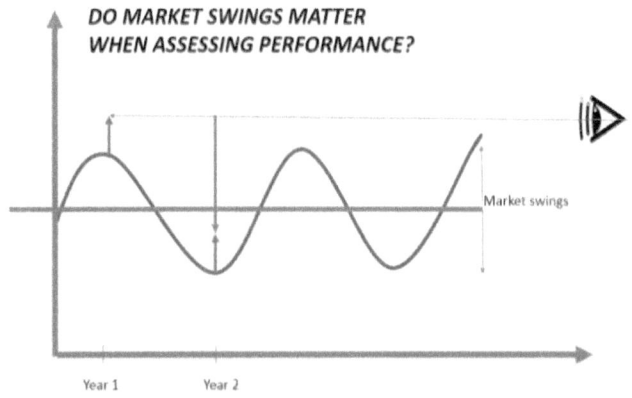

The next year, that same company grew by just 10 percent. While its employees felt that their results weren't bad, they certainly didn't feel that a celebration was justified.

But here's what the numbers didn't reveal:

In that first year of 39 percent growth, the market itself actually grew 10 percent. So in effect, the company's actual growth through its own market-independent efforts was really just 29 percent.

In that second year of "just" 10 percent growth, the market actually shrank 25 percent due to the global financial crisis—meaning that the company's actual growth through its own efforts was a stunning 35 percent!

Hence, factoring in the market's performance reveals that there was more to celebrate in the company's performance in that second year compared to its performance in the first year.

What all this simply means is: when you're assessing your employees' performance, keep the bigger picture in mind. Context really is everything.

How to Leverage the Power of Employees Through Teams

It's a fact of working life these days that the only way to produce lasting or sustainable results is by working in a team. Oddly enough, however, many organizations still haven't learned how to train their employees to work effectively as part of a team. Below is a list of key factors that can lower team energy, resulting in lower effectiveness and poorer results:

1. **Low Spirits.** Team spirit is extremely impactful on team performance and a high team spirit is often a function of high positive emotion. While it may seem odd to talk about emotions in the context of performance, all of us know that when we're in a good mood, things just go more smoothly and we accomplish a lot more compared to when we're in a bad mood.

2. **Just Doing the Job.** "Just doing the job" is the kind of attitude prevalent in command-and-control types of organizations, where employees just wait for the next order rather than think for themselves. Just doing the job means that employees don't use their brains, and, as we put it: no brain, no gain.

3. **Internal Rifts.** Internal rifts can be caused by any number of things, but two particularly common contributors are a belief in the superiority of one's team over other teams and a tendency to compete with other teams *within* the organization. While pride in one's team is a good thing, too much of it can be seriously counterproductive for the organization as a whole. Yet another source of internal conflict is the inability to handle mistakes

with emotional maturity. While mistakes are inevitable, handling them immaturely leads to even *more* mistakes. Teams that respond to the errors or failures of an individual team member with attack or criticism are prone to making even *more* errors and failures due to lower levels of collaboration and trust.

Hence, to unleash the power of employees through teams, organizations need to cultivate the kinds of conditions where true collaboration can flourish. That means, in turn, cultivating high spirits, going beyond the call of duty and powerfully addressing the sources of counterproductive conflict.

ABOUT THE AUTHORS

Bjorn Martinoff and his wife Victoria Penaflor-Martinoff are Global Chief Executive Officer and Executive Coaches who have chosen to make their home in the Philippines since 2003. Their work with the leaders and leadership teams of organizations in over 40 countries has brought their clients return on investments ranging between $1 to 11 million. Bjorn and Victoria are inspired by their belief in the infinite potential of human beings and they have worked with many of the world's Fortune 100 companies in designing and implementing organizational, human capital and leadership development solutions.

Bjorn is the author of the books *Develop Exponential Power: Stop Chasing It and Let It Chase You* and *Unstoppable Leadership and Exponential Results*. He has nearly two decades of experience in coaching top leaders and senior management teams on turning around crisis situations, accelerating business results and producing breakthrough results. He has been referred to by the Global News Network as the "Number One Global Executive Coach" and has worked with Audi, Avon, Boehringer-Ingelheim, Bristol-Myers Squibb, Citigroup, Cypress, Dell, General

Motors, IBM, Infiniti, Intel, Johnson & Johnson, Kraft, L'Oreal, La Farge, Lufthansa, Maersk, Mead-Johnson, Mercedes-Benz, Mitsubishi, Navitaire Accenture, NCO Group, Nestlé, Nissan, ON Semiconductor, Ovaltine, Pfizer, Porsche, Procter & Gamble, Samsung, San Miguel Corporation, Speedo, SunPower, Twinings, Unilab, Unilever and Volkswagen, among many others.

Victoria specializes in maximizing executive potential and performance through her coaching, consulting and training services and on-air hosting. She has over 10 years of professional and international experience in the fields of executive coaching, executive development, people development, organizational development, training design, trade and industry development and management consulting. She has worked with the Asian Development Bank, Forsspac, L'Oreal, NCO Group, Nestlé, Samsung, San Miguel, Sun Power, the Supreme Court of the Philippines, Unilever and Zoobic Safari, among others. Victoria finds meaning in helping professionals deal with performance issues in the area of career development and transition, interpersonal relationships in culturally diverse workplaces and work-life balance and fulfillment. She is adept at working with clients from different employment levels and cultural backgrounds.

You can visit Bjorn's and Victoria's websites at fortune100coach.com and flc-international.com to explore more of their work and what they make possible.

MORE PRAISE FOR UNSTOPPABLE LEADERSHIP AND EXPONENTIAL RESULTS

Celebrated coach and leadership guru Bjorn Martinoff writes with passion, utilizing his long years of experience in building successful teams, to share his definition of leadership as opposed to the traditional, top-down, "forceful" model which so captivated us in the past. He talks at length and provides guidance about how to go outside one's comfort zone to evolve as a leader...from leading oneself to leading followers, to leading peers, to leading leaders. Imagine the power and output of an organization which empowers leaders at all levels. This is an outstanding and exciting read which I strongly recommend!

Doreswamy Nandkishore
Former Chief Executive Officer of Nestlé Nutrition
and former Executive Board Member of Nestlé

The difficulty with leadership principles and ideas—and therefore with leadership books that are published every year—is that they all sound totally obvious and easy to implement as long as they sit on paper. What makes Bjorn's and Victoria's book a better book is they put together their understanding of leadership principles multiplied by their years of experience in coaching leaders at all levels in the organization. Their book not only dives into the ingredients of great leadership, but also teaches you in an admirable way how to combine them to make a great and durable impact on your organization.

Erwan Vilfeu
Chief Executive Officer of Nestlé Korea

Bravo! I thoroughly enjoyed this book! Its distinctions between management versus leadership and force versus power and its description of creating a vision, purpose and mission for the organization are all so valid and up to date! I was also captivated by its explanation of the stages in developing new leaders. It was interesting to read such a good summary of the leadership dilemmas we face day-to-day in business and the book inspired me to think about my own ways of leadership and the evolution of leadership theory and practice over the past two-and-a-half decades of my career!

Peter Noszek
Chief Executive Officer of Nestlé Hungary

MORE PRAISE FOR UNSTOPPABLE LEADERSHIP AND EXPONENTIAL RESULTS

This book is an addictive read! It demystifies leadership and translates what can be a complex topic to very simple concepts and practices. It empowers the reader to be a LEADER! This book is for everyone who wants to create positive and meaningful impact every day. It's about bringing the best version of ourselves to work and allowing leaders to bring out the best in others. It allows organizations to continue to thrive in today's disruptive world. Thank you for sharing your new book, Bjorn and Victoria!

Ira Reyes
Managing Director of Human Resources
at Accenture Philippines

Bjorn and Victoria have created a phenomenal book. Indeed, this is one of the best leadership books I have ever read. The ideas presented were thought-provoking yet grounded and practical. Their approach is engaging, interactive and reflective all at the same time. As leaders, their book propels us to revisit how our experiences forged us to become the kind of leaders we are today and how we can be better in the future—the kind of leader who can drive exponential growth, and at the end of the day, results. A must-read, I should say.

Lelie Banaglorioso
Human Resources Head at Servier Philippines

If you believe you are a leader, this book narrates your story. This humble attempt takes you step by step on what you may just be ignoring. As leaders, we are so busy with our agenda and our diaries keep us on the run. If you pause and ask "What value am I adding?" realization sets in and this is what this book will do for you. It will set you on a true path of discovering yourself.

Mehmood Khan
Social Entrepreneur and former Global Leader
of the Innovation Process at Unilever

"Unstoppable" is a fitting name to this book! Bjorn and Victoria have masterfully crafted the true essence of leadership in a concise, simple, honest and direct way. The book provides an excellent mirror and springboard for leaders to reflect on themselves as they practice what is perhaps the most important role in human history. Indeed, true leadership is the ethical use of power to create value in society, in the organization and the community of people involved in a demonstrable, repeatable and sustainable way.

Noel Lorenzana
Chief Executive Officer, Executive Chairman and Investor in Fast Moving Consumer Goods, Technology, Micro Finance and Media

Unstoppable Leadership and Exponential Results is a powerful sequel to Bjorn's book *Develop Exponential Power: Stop Chasing It and Let It Chase You*. It aptly and effectively goes back to the fundamentals of leadership and organization development, but it uses a more current lens to provide an even more relevant map for team and organizational success. Congratulations, Bjorn and Victoria! This book is an achievement!

Eric Riego de Dios
Director for Global Talent for Baker McKenzie Global Services Manila and Global Advocate for Organization Transformation and People Analytics

I find Bjorn's and Victoria's book so inspiring. It's relatable, honest and simple enough for anyone and everyone to understand. It provides tools as well as theory that will make it simple to apply its principles. I enjoyed the examples used to illustrate points more clearly. Congratulations, Bjorn and Victoria, on a successful book!!!

Jennifer Francis
Asian Development Bank

This book is bursting with powerful distinctions which could have easily filled a series of ten books on the science of success! It's an introduction to living a joyous and fulfilled life by taking a keener focus on ways to be happy while doing business moment by moment, reflecting on the lessons learned from each encounter and celebrating the daily victories which come in abundance. Bjorn and Victoria's generous compilation of experiences and expertise will turn your organization into an "unstoppable" environment where teams are relentless in fulfilling their purpose and operating at their highest performance with grace and ease.

Martina Sprangers
Human Resource Development Director of UpTBB
& Upbeat Thailand and Consultant and Trainer
at Carrying the Olive Branch

Looking for the magic formula that will make you unstoppable as a leader? You've found the right book. Bjorn and Victoria Martinoff share a fresh approach to leadership in an engaging, human and practical way. Learn how to differentiate between power and force and use power to build bridges of trust and not ditches of distrust with force. Join Bjorn and Victoria on a journey of leadership discovery and you too will become "unstoppable."

Scott Friedman
Author, Former President
of the National Speakers Association and
Co-Founder of "Together We Can Change the World"

In a world that is unprecedentedly changing, to grow is not enough—one has to exponentially grow oneself and the organization. Bjorn and Victoria offer insightful thoughts on how to harness the energy in leadership that brings exponential results. Oftentimes, organizations are so focused on their business strategies that they neglect the true source of power—people! Be guided by the insights here and build your true competitive advantage.

Ringo Morella
Human Resources Director
at Mead Johnson Nutrition Canada

It was a deep source of inspiration for me to read this book. By writing his first book, *Develop Exponential Power: Stop Chasing It and Let It Chase You*, and then its sequel, Bjorn has gifted humankind with a remarkable set of guidelines on personal transformation and a stirring inspiration to becoming better on a daily basis.

Dina Loomis
President of the Southeast Asia Speakers
and Trainers Bureau

Bjorn's and Victoria's book has the logic, frameworks, methodologies, "whys" of leading and managing, and wisdom molded on the credible track record of experiences of the authors. They have deployed time-tested formulas that will propel anyone to be "unstoppable" in inspiring, motivating, persuading, developing and empowering anybody to be the best that they can be, to become "fruitful" and not just successful in their endeavors, and to use their roles purposely for the greater glory of God!

Roberto Policarpio
Former President of the People Management
Association of the Philippines

This book speaks about leading "human beings," not just using that term as another word for "people." Instead it highlights the importance of actual being, i.e., being connected, being significant and being certain of one's place and role. Helping one's self and one's colleagues and co-workers achieve that sense of being leads to extraordinary results. Bjorn and Victoria provide us with tips and techniques that can be put into practice right away, with virtually immediate return on investment. I am already adapting these tips into my style!

Stephen Cutler, PhD
Director of the Guide Meridian Company

This book elevates consciousness on many powerful concepts. Bjorn has spent years thinking about the concepts of force and power and spent two more years writing about them in a book that is dedicated to showing us what makes force and power so different. Bjorn then moves into teaching us how to use our new understanding of force and power to better lead our lives and our organizations towards exponential growth, fulfilling success...and eventually becoming, in Bjorn's words, "unstoppable." It's an empowering read right from the introduction which I loved.

Michael Kouly
Author, Global Leadership Thinker and President and Chief Executive Officer of the Cambridge Institute for Global Leadership

This book gives you cutting-edge yet practical, realistic and valuable insights on how to fast-track yourself into being a purpose-driven leader who can drive tremendous positive change and transformation in people and organizations. The authors in my mind have truly established themselves as thought leaders.

Grace Chan Hwee
Senior General Manager of Group Human Resource and Administration at the Berjaya Corporation Berhad

I have been working for the past 25 years with more than 20 chief executive officers in America, Asia and Europe and helping them achieve disproportionate growth in sales and earnings. It has been possible only through the clarity of purpose, values and vision and the power of persuasion and effective collaboration that celebrates diversity. I was very excited when I recently discovered that Bjorn and Victoria have beautifully and effectively elaborated these concepts in their book using the metaphor of power versus force. I recommend this book to anyone who wants to take their leadership to the next level!

Anand Sharma
Founder and Chief Executive Officer
of the Growth Advisory and Founding Board Member
of the South East Asia Leadership Academy

In this book, Bjorn and Victoria share the latest and most cutting-edge strategies and stages of leadership growth, how growth is measured and how true growth always happens outside of your comfort zone. The Martinoffs also share the evolutionary stages in developing leaders, what can slow your leadership team down and how to change that. There are many gems in this book including the wonderful use of stories and quotes from other thought leaders. It will be an instant classic for anyone who wants to fast forward their leadership and develop exponential results!

Kimberley Barker, PhD
Director for the Institute for Culture
and Adaptive Leadership

Bjorn's views on leadership are born out of his review of the literature, his discussions with leaders and his keen observations of leadership dynamics in organizations. The leadership aspects he espouses point to practical applications of the principles. While the leadership author Joseph Rost reviewed literature on leadership written over two centuries, Bjorn both studied the literature and surveyed people and insightfully came up with his own views of leadership and power. His book is a work I can refer to over and over again as it serves as an effective being-oriented and results-oriented guide to authentic leadership.

Raul Rodriguez, PhD
Professor at the John Gokongwei School of Management of the Ateneo de Manila University

The Martinoffs' latest book is amazingly spot-on. I find the deep insights and takeaway advice the keys to realizing a leadership operating model that will define sustainable success. Leaders who ignore Bjorn's and Victoria's views and perspectives do so at their own risk and peril! I sincerely hope that this book will be a catalyst to further propagate Bjorn's and my shared advocacy of leadership excellence across the private, public and civil society spaces in the Philippines, South East Asia and beyond.

Ramon Segismundo
Chief Human Resources Officer at the Manila Electric Company

Leadership is powerful when it truly empowers. Bjorn and Victoria provide simple and practical pointers on taking leadership capabilities to the next level!

Dean Aragon
Chief Executive Officer of Shell Brands International and Global VP Brand for Shell

There is so much noise and so many voices on the subject matter of leadership. Bjorn and Victoria sift through the noise and present a rational voice on leadership lessons in this book. Leadership is such a delicate and important subject matter that it should not be presented or commented upon by people who do not have the depth of knowledge and wisdom to comment on it. But Bjorn and Victoria have this depth and this is why this book presents a must-read for people who want to study, know and learn more about the intricate features of leadership.

Francis Kong
Author, Speaker, Trainer and Entrepreneur

Bjorn is brilliant. There's wisdom in every page of his book. If you're leading your team and you need clear guidance for the tough decisions you need to make, this book has the answers.

Bo Sanchez
Bestselling Author

It takes the highest level of skill and patience to deliver the bad news of your fundamental leadership flaws to you. Bjorn does this with a gentler and more caring heart than anyone I know.

Jeff Thanatkrit Malhotra
Executive and Performance Coach

I agree wholeheartedly with Bjorn and Victoria that the 6+1 imperatives of employee engagement go hand in hand with the successful acceptance of the vision and purpose.

Roddy Abaya
Vice President and Division Human Resources Manager at San Miguel Pure Foods

This book reminds us that while the world is changing at ever-faster speeds, the fundamental principles of leadership are still as relevant as ever. This book is a very useful reminder for seasoned leaders and an excellent step-by-step guide for aspiring leaders and leaders that want to elevate their game.

Bruno Olierhoek
Managing Director at Nestlé
Pakistan and Afghanistan

The book written by Bjorn and Victoria is one of the must-read books for business leaders who want to transform from the traditional command-and-control paradigm to the current one based on respect and sharing. The authors have many years of coaching senior leaders around the world and they have gotten insights from their work in dealing with them. As a global chief executive coach, their book will help other business leaders understand the management transformation process better. If you are looking for the reasons, consequences and solutions of transforming either yourself or a leadership team, this book is for you.

Laurence Yap
Human Resources and
Organizational Development Leader

This exceptional book challenges the role of a leader in the new age. It uncovers how you can unleash your potential, maximize your leadership power and deliver results with passion and purpose. Thank you, Bjorn and Victoria, for allowing me to realize the new definition of leadership that is not forceful but inspiring. This is a must-read book—very grounded and inspiring in setting one's leadership ahead of the race!

Engelbert Camasura
President at Asia Select and
Education Partner at the Society
for Human Resources Management Philippines

Definitions of leadership are as plentiful as the number of authors on the topic, but this does not diminish the importance of developing leaders, especially in today's disruptive environment. Bjorn's and Victoria's book cuts through the clutter and gives the reader clear frameworks and examples on how to "be and do" leadership. This is an essential guide for those who are leading teams, those aspiring to lead organizations and those coaching upcoming leaders. Exploring concepts such as power, engagement and the vectoring force of team dynamics, this book has answers for those committed to self-leadership and effectively leading others.

Andrew Bryant
Author, Speaker and Executive Coach

Bjorn and Victoria sum up how the unlimited power we discover from within ourselves and our teams may be measured quantitatively and qualitatively to our advantage. As opposed to using pure force in simply managing our resources and affairs, power and leadership are an indispensable duo in any organization. Bjorn and Victoria can save us from the most common pitfalls in running our operations, especially when realized at a much earlier stage. Their book is another gentle guide in my own journey as a catalyst of change and betterment in my own business and organizations!

Michelle Lucas
Chief Executive Officer and Entrepreneur

I highly recommend this book for both current and aspiring leaders. Bjorn has once again provided a road map on how to transform oneself from being just ordinary to becoming highly successful! His book will surely help anyone looking to make an impact on their organization or planning to take their career to greater heights.

Darwin Rivers
Founder and Executive President
of the Philippines HR Group

This book is for the organizational professional and for anyone who is serious about their career growth in management. The distinction between force and power brings the reader present to a useful and thought-provoking background conversation. Informed by Dr. David Dawkins' seminal work *Power vs. Force*, Bjorn and Victoria revivify this crucial inquiry into the nature of power. Their book can and should be read on several levels and will tend to stimulate thinking about things which would be smart to revisit!

John King
Bestselling Author

Bjorn and Victoria Martinoff have successfully conveyed their decades of consulting experience in a way that is truly accessible. Their brilliant book gives business leaders a comprehensive yet straightforward way to develop a winning plan. I thank them for their insight and their accessible roadmap for becoming a world-class performer who inspires others through the brilliantly explained concept of power rather than force! Leaders and aspiring leaders, read it and let it help you exponentially grow your business!

Patrick Tete
Managing Director of Servier Egypt

Bjorn's and Victoria's book couldn't have come at a better timing for me as I gear up to lead leaders in transforming a century-old organization and catapulting it to where it wants to be. Their pragmatic approaches to the classic concepts of identifying purpose and vision, the importance of engaging employees as well as overcoming barriers to exponential transformation are priceless and accessible tools that I can use to ensure success in my projects as a talent management professional!

Laurice Macapaz
People and Organizational Development Expert
and Life-Long Learner

This book is another masterpiece by Bjorn and Victoria! It is certainly a must-read for every leader at all levels of their organization regardless of years of experience. Reading through the book gave me a great opportunity to learn, relearn and at the same time unlearn ways of being, thinking and doing. The core of this book is cultivating habitual ways of being and doing that harness, direct and amplify genuine power towards effective leadership and desired results. I look forward to being a witness and beneficiary of the next collaboration of the Martinoffs!

Alfie Suarez
Human Resources Director for DXC Technology
Asia, Middle East and Africa

Bjorn's and Victoria's book speaks to leaders with clarity, transparency and authenticity. It's a rare combination that is educating, engaging and inspiring for every leader who wants to be unstoppable as a leadership role model who achieves results and inspires more leaders. The book is simple yet profoundly delivered with visuals, stories and relevant content for every leader in taking them to the next level of growth and success. I highly recommended it!

Gautam Ganglani
Managing Director
of the Right Selection Speakers Bureau

Reading Bjorn's book is like going to a one-stop shop on being a leader. It's a synthesis of one man's understanding and discovery of what the exercise of leadership is and what it takes to be a leader. If reading 30,000 books on leadership is a challenge, read this book as it is perhaps one of the few essential reads that you will ever need to guide you in your quest of being an "unstoppable" leader!

Tony Galvez
Leadership Coach

Bjorn and Victoria brilliantly capture the essence of leadership by simply and clearly articulating what power really is versus force and identifies the benefits and drawbacks of each approach. They're also 1,000 percent right that leaders overuse force to achieve their corporate goals in a way that drives down employee engagement, productivity and long-term results. They also outline the key principles so leaders can easily use power that enhances the human spirit so that leaders, organizations and individuals can reach their goals in a highly advanced and humanistic manner. I will be recommending this book to my clients and peers globally!

Michael Milbier
Executive Coach and
Global Organizational Development Consultant

I've had the great fortune to work with world-class leaders and every one of them always did what was in their power to make their teams successful. Recognition, rewards and advancement were never a factor and yet, ironically, these followed them all as they rose to the most senior ranks. In the end, it has been the tenacity, grit and humility of leaders like the ones described by Bjorn and Victoria in their wonderful work that attracted followers like me. For those aspiring to be leaders one day or those already in such roles, this is a great primer and refresher!

Hans Montenegro
Chief Operations Officer
of IT Delivery Centers Asia at Manulife

While it is unfortunate that many leaders unduly use force, Bjorn's and Victoria's book auspiciously provides the means for leaders to transform towards habitually using power, which enables them to develop exponential power teams. As Bjorn and Victoria point out, this can only be done by focusing both on one's beingness and on doing.

Arthur Luis Florentin
Executive Director IV at the Civil Service Institute
of the Civil Service Commission of the Philippines

I love this book! I like that Bjorn started with beingness because the self is the ground zero of leadership. If you can't empower yourself, you can forget about empowering others. I like that the book builds on the distinction between power versus force introduced in Bjorn' previous work and provides a more detailed roadmap to increasing power. Lastly, I love that I can relate with the ideas in this book. The number of times I said "I agree!" while reading this book is a testament to how much, well, I agree with it. Bjorn, you did it again!

Edwin Ebreo
President at ExeQserve and Organizational Development and Training Consultant

Being a successful leader is challenging. It involves concepts spread across commerce, economics, psychology and many more. This book cleverly pulls together all of the components, using concepts most will understand to illustrate them, while intermingling the critical themes of leadership character. Digestible, succinct and well-focused, it should be compulsory reading for everyone interested in true leadership!

Martin Telfer
Senior Vice President and EMEA Chief at Fulcrum Global Technologies

www.ingramcontent.com/pod-product-compliance
Lightning Source LLC
Chambersburg PA
CBHW020949230426
43666CB00005B/235